MICHEL SALAMOLARD
JEAN-LOYS ORY

The art of being a catechist

Giving the WORD to children

Illustrations by
Charles-Henri Salamolard

ST PAULS

Original title: *Le métier de catéchiste*

Translated by Florestine Audette
Cover photograph: Charles-Henri Salamolard

ST PAULS
Middlegreen, Slough SL3 6BT, United Kingdom
Moyglare Road, Maynooth, Co. Kildare, Ireland

ISBN 085439 467 2

Printed by Biddles Ltd, Guildford

ST PAULS is an activity of the priests and brothers of the Society of St Paul who proclaim the Gospel through the media of social communication

THE ART OF BEING A CATECHIST

CONTENTS

Chapters marked with an asterisk (*) are particularly suitable for a first reading.

Preface

Being a catechist today is an important mission, entrusted to us by Christ, and which must be assumed by priests and laypersons together.

Being a catechist today is also a task difficult to accomplish in a world subject to constant mutation, where the most diverse and contradictory ideas and convictions are in perpetual confrontation.

Being a catechist today is also a source of immense joy, as one becomes aware of the wonders performed by God in the hearts of children, young people and adults. It is also the source of a personal renewal in faith.

But discouragement easily follows a generous commitment if an adapted formation and a personal companionship do not sustain and reinforce the initial enthusiasm.

This book by Fr Michel Salamolard and Fr Jean-Loys Ory will be a precious means of formation and will foster sharing in dialogue with colleagues. Clearly, it has its place in the concerted effort displayed in recent years, prompted and supported by the Commission for catechesis in French-speaking Switzerland, to elaborate and set up a plan and framework of catechesis. This book calls for other documents to be put in the hands of catechists to allow them to fulfil their mission better. Besides, the actual multiplicity of textbooks for children does not make the application of the plan and framework any easier. The elaboration of textbooks linked with this plan appears to be increasingly necessary.

The constant preoccupation of the authors is to help catechists live their faith in greater depth, to allow them always to have a better grasp of what is at stake, of the goals and methods of catechesis while remaining faithful to the major guidelines given by the universal Church.

Already more than fifty years ago, a professor of pedagogy of the University of Fribourg, Mgr E. Dévaud, pointed out that the purpose of catechesis is not primarily to provide knowledge but to develop a life, to promote Christian attitudes. Knowledge, surely indispensable, must be at the service of the life with and in Christ. The constant concern of catechists must be to make Jesus Christ known so that the children, young people and adults they are addressing may, enlivened by his Spirit, live a new life from him and with him. That is why, in catechesis, it is important to address the whole person, and not only his or her intelligence, through activities that challenge all the faculties of the human person. And the first 'activity', beyond any doubt, is silent prayer; it ought to make a personal contact with God, the encounter with and the discovery of a God who loves us, possible.

If we want to avoid a divorce between faith and life, it is important to place the two in constant correlation, that is, the faith and the human experience of each, the faith and the Christian experience of each, the faith and the life of the Church. Faithful to the fundamental intuition of the plan and framework, the authors hope to bring about a better understanding of this basic principle of 'correlation'.

'I have come so that you may have life and have it abundantly,' Jesus told us. May this book help the catechists and its readers understand better, and make others understand, that, as the baptized, we are called to live a new life, a life in Christ, a life of love of God and of others. We are called to live, in depth with God, all the personal, familial, social and political aspects of our life as a human being. According to the beautiful words of St Ignatius of Antioch in the second century, we are called to 'imitate the moral principles of God'.

This is the fiery message that we, the catechists of today, must proclaim, first by living it, to those entrusted to us in catechesis. Our thanks to Michel Salamolard and Jean-Loys Ory for helping us to achieve this.

+ Gabriel Bullet
Bishop Auxiliary
Delegate of the bishops of
French-speaking Switzerland for catechesis

Open letter to the reader

Dear friend,

Allow us to address you in this way for, if you read this book, there already exists a shared and secret understanding between us. As catechists, parents, Christian educators, our common project is to transmit the word to the children, our word and that of God, all in the same motion. In order that these children we love may in turn speak and tell God and us what they are, what they live and what they believe.

By offering you this book on pedagogy, we hope to join you in your desire to give the best to the children entrusted to your care. We hope to facilitate your task by revealing a few secrets about the 'duty' you already fulfil with competence and love.

By doing this work in pedagogy, we also hope to contribute in a modest way to the proof that a catechesis, or a well understood religious instruction, has its place in an educative project nourished with Christian references.

We thank you for your trust and we wish you a pleasant and profitable read.

Michel Salamolard
Jean-Loys Ory
Charles-Henri Salamolard

Introduction

This book was born from a concern and a hope. In the social and cultural context of Western Europe, catechesis and evangelization represent a challenge. The Churches have understood that: everywhere a remarkable investment is being made in catechesis. The catechists, sustained by a generally effective organization, are numerous. However, the demands and the needs are such that, often, the formation does not measure up to the goodwill.

Now a sound training is essential. It is demanding. Serious efforts have already been made to give the catechists the material and equipment which is absolutely necessary for them to deepen their own faith and to progress in their lives as Christians. In fact, we educate by starting from what we are. Nevertheless, in many regions, formation remains elementary, fragmentary and incomplete. Such is the concern we share with other Christians who are responsible for the catechetical formation.

The reasons which explain this situation are diverse: lack of time and means, the scope of the task. It has also appeared to us, in the course of our practical work, that a tool for formation was lacking: a textbook of catechetical pedagogy. There obviously exist excellent works written by experts, but they are presented rather as a theory of the catechetical act and offer few means for its concrete application. Or again, practical elements exist but in a dispersed state, in periodicals or in the introductions to different itineraries and programmes.

What has motivated us, therefore, is our concern to contribute to the initiative of training catechists by making available to them a study, both sound and practical, which examines all the principal questions that emerge in the catechetical activity.

Our hope is that this work may stimulate, reinforce and facilitate the efforts in formation already in progress and give rise to new ones. That is why we have planned our textbook in the perspective that it might be used by a formation team. Far from replacing or making the existing devices of formation superfluous, our book supposes their existence and refers to them. Not that a private use of this book might be impossible, but its benefits would be thus greatly reduced. In any case, an eminently catechetical element would be lacking: the experience of the Church community, a place of formation par excellence.

Our starting point is that of our experience, as much in the catechesis itself as in the formation of catechists. We have had the privilege of being in contact with children, young people and adults, all of whom being much different in their personal, family or social situations. It is with them and thanks to them that we have progressively better understood what catechesis is. It is with gratitude that we dedicate this book to them.

Our gratitude is equally extended to the persons and the colleagues who have encouraged us to publish this textbook. The first one in mind is Mgr Gabriel Bullet whose trust proved to be decisive. Our thanks also to the friends of Provence – the Community of Baume-läs-Aix, Anne-Marie and the Carmelite Sisters of Aix-en-Provence – who offered us the material, friendly and spiritual environment for our work.

Our thanks to Fr Michel Maret who assumed the re-reading of our manuscript.

Finally, we benefited from a most friendly understanding on the part of our editors, the Sisters of the Work of Saint Augustine, to whom we extend our warm and sincere thanks.

Three axes of formation

The initial and permanent formation of the catechists is developed in three interconnected areas:

1. *A spiritual growth.* To discover oneself as a person and as a daughter or son of God, to accept one's limitations and status as a sinner in order to receive oneself as infinitely loved: it is the very becoming of oneself which is at stake here. This line of growth, the most decisive one, is favoured by prayer, by the active participation in the life of the Church, by the help of a competent companion.

2. *A theological formation.* Based on the knowledge of, and on the attentive listening to the Word of God and its appropriation, its aim is to understand, in a vital and personal way, the 'mystery of faith', the truth about man and his destiny, the truth about God. It is not a matter of being learned nor of accumulating a body of abstract knowledge, but to receive the light of Revelation, the latter's capacity to enlighten our existence, and to be able to give an account of it in a simple and precise language.

3. *A pedagogical formation.* This allows the personal attitudes and talents to bear fruit and give their full measure.

Our textbook is concerned with the pedagogical axis. Nevertheless, we have planned it from a perspective which, we hope, will incite the reader to grow spiritually and deepen his or her faith.

Presentation and Method

As its title indicates, the goal of this textbook is to facilitate the learning process of the 'art' of catechetics. What does catechesis consist of? Why and how should it be exercised? These are the questions we wish to answer.

This book, therefore, does not take the place of the itineraries or programmes proper to each age group and region. It is, we believe, their useful complement.

In the first part, sections I and II, we explain precisely what catechesis is, what are its aims and relation to the Christian experience, what is its place in the life and mission of the Church.

In the second part, sections III to VI, we deal with the different facets of catechetical pedagogy, in its practical use as in its justifications at the theological level or at the level of humanities.

Each chapter includes two elements: some information and some appropriation exercises. This means that our study supposes that the reader will do some work on his own. Work in terms of reading: we have attempted to make this easier by using a simple language without being simplistic. Work in terms of appropriation through the exercises suggested. This twofold approach will bear all its fruit if, as we indicated in the introduction, it is carried out by a formation team, accompanied by an experienced and competent person.

Our study is equipped with different materials which will make its use easier. The table of contents offers an overall view of the topics treated. The index of themes allows one to find rapidly the places where the same theme is approached from different points of view. This index can also be used as a glossary: the technical or difficult words are listed with a reference to the pages where a definition or an explanation of the terms may be found.

We have been particularly careful about the illustrating of our book. To us – there is no mistake about it – it is not only an ornament but an integral part of the study. It will make the importance and the role of the image in pedagogy more readily understood than would a theory.

As it is, this book does not necessarily require that a linear reading of it be made from the first to the last page. You can enter into its content through the door of any chapter and pursue, according to your needs and interests, the one or the other itinerary suggested by the marginal notes and other references. It is equally possible to exploit a particular line of thought by consulting the thematic index.

As a guideline and by way of introduction, we suggest that you begin with the chapters marked with an asterisk (*) in the table of contents, putting the others on hold for a deeper study.

We have experienced much joy in putting together this book about formation. We have laboured with utmost care in the keen hope that this work will not only be a worthwhile study but a pleasant one as well. In spite of that, we are very aware that there is room for greater perfection in our textbook. Consequently, we will gratefully accept any remarks and suggestions apt to improve it.

Even if, in this study, our sights are set on catechesis for children, a large part of what we are suggesting has a wider scope and, with proper adaptations, can be used in faith journeys with adolescents, young people and adults.

List of abbreviations

The biblical books are quoted according to the current abbreviation system of the Revised Standard Version (RSV).

AA *Apostolicam Actuositatem*, Decree on the apostolate of lay people, Vatican II

CT *Catechesis Tradendae*, Exhortation on catechesis in our time by John Paul II, 1979

GCD *General Catechetical Directory*, Sacred Congregation of the Clergy, 1971

DV *Dei Verbum*, Dogmatic Constitution on divine Revelation, Vatican II, 1965

EN *Evangelii Nuntiandi*, Exhortation on evangelization in the modern world by Paul VI, 1975

LG *Lumen Gentium*, Dogmatic Constitution on the Church, Vatican II, 1964

Note: Excerpts from papal documents are quoted from Austin Flannery, OP, general editor, *Vatican Council II*, Volume I, New revised edition, 1992; Volume II, 1982, Liturgical Press, Collegeville, Indiana, U.S.A.

For Anne-Gabrielle Steiner

1. At the heart of life, a question: God? Man?

We never reach man separated from language and we never see him in the process of inventing it. It is a speaking man that we find in the world, a man speaking to another man and the language teaches the definition of man.

E. Benveniste, *Problèmes de linguistique générale*, p. 259, Gallimard 1966.

Life, like a grammar... I-you-he (she)-we-you...they!
Verbs-Subjects-Objects!
Space, time, time-space.
Numbers and letters.
The sun, the stars.
Man, his story in the history of men. His birth... his death...

Man grappling with the world, to understand it,
to free himself from it,
because the world and he 'make two'.

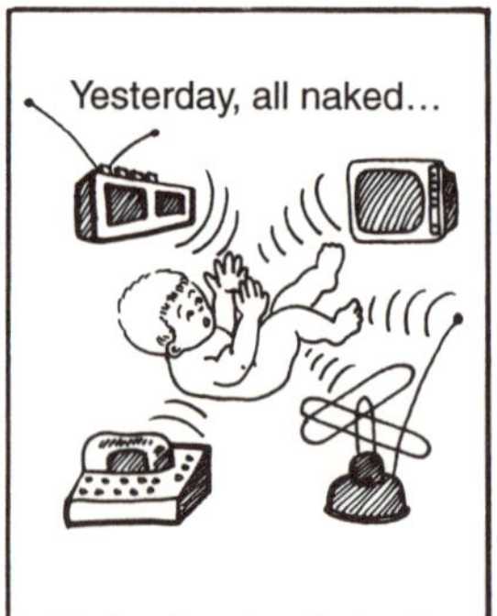

Today, bombarded with audiovisual messages

Heaven, where is that?

One wonders...

So, he doesn't exist!

Man who speaks and remains silent. Who smiles and weeps. Who grows and declines.
Man who opens himself in love and shuts himself off in despair.
Man who prays before his mirror or before a cross.
Man who 'is in pursuit of himself' with his conscience.
Man who is man and woman, and family, and group and nation, and culture.
Man who brings himself into the world of freedom and fills prisons.
Man who is not perfected, and who still and always wonders 'how' and 'why', and 'for whom'.
Man who never comes to the end of misconstruing things, who cannot put up with nonsense,

he wants to believe that everything has a meaning...
otherwise, nothing has any sense!

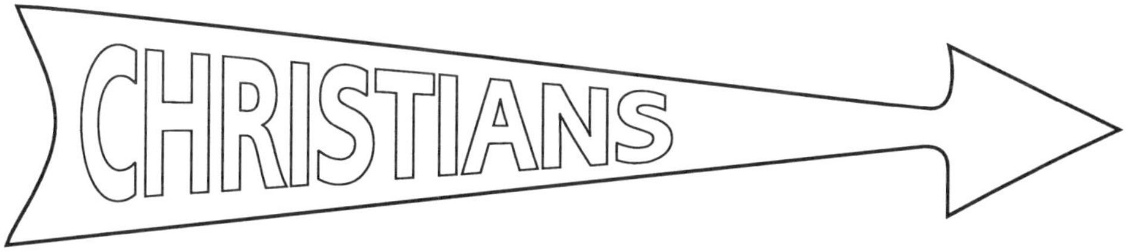

Appropriation

1. Among the illustrations of this chapter, choose the one most meaningful to you. What does it tell you? What does it make you think of?
2. Suppose God is asking you, personally, one question. What would it be... insofar as you know him? And your answer? Share with the group.

AND WHAT IF THE QUESTION WERE IN GOD...
AND THE ANSWER IN MAN?

2. A broad perspective: The history of salvation

Blessed be the God and Father of our Lord Jesus Christ, who has blessed us in Christ with every spiritual blessing in the heavenly places, just as he chose us in Christ before the foundation of the world to be holy and blameless before him in love.

He destined us for adoption as his children through Jesus Christ, according to the good pleasure of his will, to the praise of his glorious grace that he freely bestowed on us in the Beloved.

In him we have redemption through his blood, the forgiveness of our trespasses, according to the riches of his grace that he lavished on us.

With all wisdom and insight he has made known to us the mystery of his will, according to his good pleasure that he set forth in Christ, as a plan for the fullness of time, to gather up all things in him, things in heaven and things on earth.

In Christ we have also obtained an inheritance, having been destined according to the purpose of him who accomplishes all things according to his counsel and will, so that we, who were the first to set our hope on Christ, might live for the praise of his glory.

In him you also, when you had heard the word of truth, the gospel of your salvation, and had believed in him, were marked with the seal of the promised Holy Spirit; this is the pledge of our inheritance toward redemption as God's own people, to the praise of his glory.

Eph 1:3-14

A history in history proclaims God as the beyond of all history

A MYSTERY, indeed... like God! But which revealed itself to the heart of men. And they have engraved it in their own history:

Israel, JESUS, the Church

We can re-read this revelation today in the faith and history of these two nations of the Covenant, the Old fulfilled in the New: 'I have come not to abolish but to fulfil' (Mt 5:17). Through the faith and the events that stand out as milestones in the particular history of a people, this revelation is progressive and moving toward a salvation of which it proclaims the promise; it culminates at a 'propitious time': 'Jesus [was] proclaiming the goods news of God, and saying, "The time is fulfilled, and the kingdom of God has come near"' (Mk 1:14-15); and it leads us to a narrative.

> Between the real or experienced history and history as a science, there must be another form of history, the history as tradition or the history as a narrative. Whereas history as a science reconstructs the past in discontinuity with this past – or starting from what we call an 'epistemological cut' – history as tradition or an account is a re-reading of it in the present and for the present. It means that the history of the past always acts on the present, not only in the sense that the present prolongs the past, but in the sense that it finds in it the understanding of what is happening to it. Thus, Israel, particularly in the troubled periods of its history, evokes the 'mighty deeds' of God through which it discovers what God means to it still today. If it is a matter, for instance, of expressing that the love of God is eternal, that this love is still active today, we cannot do so by offering an abstract definition of God or love, but by telling how this love manifested itself in concrete ways since the beginning.
>
> A. Dartigues, p. 177

God the Son became man so that we might become sons of God

God the Son became man so that we might become sons of God

God the Son became man so that we might become sons of God

We have let St Paul himself present God's plan to you. You will find the same thing, in different forms, as you recite the Apostles' Creed, as you re-read the documents of the Church, for example, LG 2.

Since the object of catechesis embraces the whole content of this plan (= REVELATION), we limit ourselves by giving you here only the capital letters of this mystery:

Trinity

Just as Christ is the centre of salvation history, so the mystery of God is the centre from which this mystery originated and towards which it is ordained as to its final end. The crucified and risen Christ leads people to the Father by sending the Spirit to God's People. For this reason, the structure of the entire content of catechesis must be theocentric-trinitarian: through Christ, to the Father, in the Spirit. GCD 41

Incarnation

Since Christ Jesus, Word of God Incarnate, is the ultimate reason why God intervened in the world and showed himself to people, he is the centre of the gospel message in salvation history… For this reason, catechesis must necessarily be Christocentric. GCD 40

Redemption

The theocentric-trinitarian purpose of the economy of salvation cannot be separated from its objective, which is to free people from sin and its consequences and to make them as much like Christ as possible (cf LG 39). Every revealed truth, like the incarnation of the Word, is for us people and for our salvation. GCD 42

Ecclesial body

Since the Church is not merely the people of God but also, as it were, in Christ 'a sign and instrument... of communion with God and of unity among all men' (LG 1), it should be regarded as the primordial sacrament. GCD 55

God the Son became man so that we might become sons of God

> And what about
> CREATION?
> Read,
> and meditate!

Already in the Old Testament, the truth of God's creative power is not put forward as an abstract philosophical principle, but gains entry into the minds of the Israelites with the help of the concept of the unity of God, as a proclamation of Yahweh's power and victory, as demonstration that God always stands by his people (cf Isa 40:27-28; 51:9-13). The omnipotence of God the creator is most clearly manifested in Christ's resurrection, in which is revealed 'how vast are the resources of his power' (Eph 1:19).

Consequently, the truth of creation is not to be put forward simply as a truth standing on its own, artificially separated from the rest, but as something which is in fact related to the salvation won by Jesus Christ. The creation of things visible and invisible, of the world and of angels, is the commencement of the history of salvation (cf DV 3); the creation of man (cf Pius XII, Enc. Humani generis, 1950; GS 12, 14) is to be regarded as the first gift and the first call leads to glorification in Christ (cf Rom 8:29-30). GCD 51

Appropriation

1. You are asked one question: 'And what about creation?' Can you place it within the framework of the four 'capital letters' of the Christian mystery?
2. Catechesis and creation: in your opinion, is there a kinship or bond between these two realities?

3. The Church –
People in communion

Take your Bible and read Acts of the Apostles 2:42-47. Let yourselves be amazed:
- who are the actors?
- who is the one acting?

Then go back to the previous chapter, 'TIRE': after the Father, the Son, the Holy Spirit... THE CHURCH

PEOPLE OF GOD* BODY OF CHRIST* TEMPLE OF THE SPIRIT*

GCD 55-59

The primordial sacrament GCD 67
The salvation sacrament GCD 66, 68, 69
Communion

How can we affirm this?

(a) Jesus alone is mediator. THROUGH HIM {God reveals and gives himself DV 2
{We have access to God (cf Heb) GCD 12

He is the priest of the New Covenant, as he is also the shepherd. In the sense of God-man and in the sense of man-God, he is the author of salvation and he realizes it. Thus we can say: Jesus is the sacrament of God: the one who makes and who signifies salvation, and he does so superabundantly. GCD 50, 54

Through Him, with Him and in Him, in the unity of the Spirit, all glory and honour is yours, almighty Father, forever and ever. Amen.

(b) '... I have made known to you everything that I have heard from my Father' (Jn 15:15). 'As the Father has loved me, so I have loved you' (Jn 15:9; 17:23). 'As the Father has sent me, so I send you' (Jn 17:18; 20:21). '... so that the love with which you have loved me may be in them, and I in them' (Jn 17:26). As the Body of Christ, the Church participates in this unique priesthood of Jesus, and as a member of the Church, every Christian has this power of revealing the love of God, of loving and of giving his life for those he loves, as Jesus did. In this sense, we can say that the Church is the sacrament of Christ. Her mission is to proclaim Jesus Christ to the world, to lead men to the Father and to offer them the sacraments: these signs, these gestures, these actions by which Jesus places his brothers and sisters in the presence of his Father. We can call her a primordial sacrament, and, entrusted with the task of bringing all men of all cultures and of all times to God, she is a sacrament of salvation.

* People: Jer 31:31-34 (cf 1 Cor 11:25)
* Body: 1 Cor 10:16-17 12, 27
* Temple: Eph 2:20-22 1 Cor 3:16-17

(c) Beyond this sacramental dimension which is so important in the eyes of the Church, there is a divine truth: We are always saved by an Other.

We receive ourselves from an Other. It is God symbolized at the same time as the Gift. As opposed to the sin we call original. Here, God is found again, God-with-us, and we, men- with-him: he, giving us to be men; we, acknowledging
GCD 62 him as our God who has loved us so much. Love is what is original, and not sin!

GCD 58 (d) It is always that reality that is given to us to live in the sacraments of the Church through the ordained ministry. Eminently in the Eucharist.

The priest, first a member among others of the community, is called and sacramentally ordained to represent Christ. He makes him present by being, through his person, the sign that Jesus is the saviour of the community. This 'mediation' of the priest actualizes the unique mediation of Jesus in the present-day of our history. Here, we touch the heart of the mystery of the faith of the Church and the summit of her existence. The bishop, the successor to the Apostles, is the one who lays hands to ordain the priests. Thus, the Church shows that she receives herself from Christ of whom she is the 'body' and the 'bride' (Eph 1:22-23; 5:31-32).

MISSION of Evangelization, of Sanctification, of Pastoral Leadership in the Church

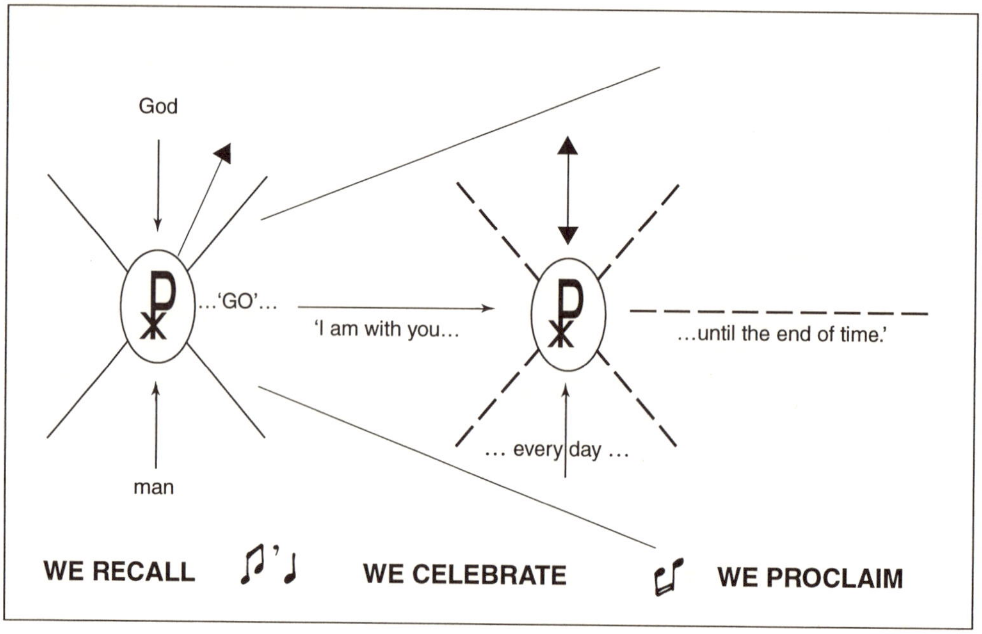

Appropriation

1. We sometimes say that the Church has a 'trinitarian' nature. After reading this chapter, has this expression become meaningful to you?
2. In your own words, express what the above sketch means to you.

4. Churches of other denominations – A common testimony

The Christian ought to leave fewer traces behind him and more ahead of him...
J. Debruynne, *Naître*, p. 80.

It is a fact: Christians have come to the point of building steeples to stand out from the others, and we were born in this accomplished fact. But we are not quits for all that: far from it!

Simply, because we are baptized, both the recipients and the bearers of the Gospel, conscious that we belong to the Church, living in the stimulating proximity of brothers and sisters of other denominations, already suffering with them from the crippling indifference of so many baptized, we are called to render an account for the hope that the Lord has placed in our hearts (1 Pet 3:15).[1]

We do this, through three practical attitudes:

– By looking to the past, we move ahead backwards: this is most inconvenient! And then, we risk bypassing what is happening to us today: try decoding the signs of the times by turning your back to them! Christ has come, he is to come: our faith is thwarted if it does not wait for him. His prayer remains at the heart of the Church set on her way.
– Let us not cast our differences in concrete, but convinced that our fidelity to Jesus Christ necessarily brings us to a convergence of faith, we will let go of our fears. Nourished at the same sources for a common destiny, we will become familiar with each other!
– Finally, for us, the 'TODAY' of salvation is now. The lever for the conversion of the world is: 'so that the world may believe'; our ecclesial testimony cannot help but 'feel' the Lord who is assembling us in his Presence:

May they be one, as we are one,
I in them and you in me (Jn 17:22-23)

1. We do not invite you to a facile ecumenism but to a demanding and hopeful one. So many things can be done, professed and prayed in common! Catechesis is certainly a privileged place to meet in the 'communion of differences'.

Appropriation

1. In your opinion, how may catechesis contribute to an ecumenical rapprochement? By being faithful to what demands?
2. From this point of view, how does the situation in your region present itself? What do you think of it?

5. Christian existence

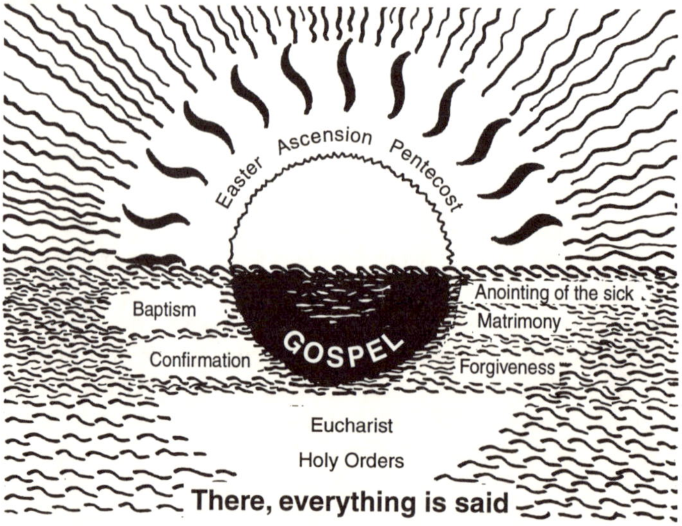

Modern people would say:

planning?	competitiveness?
marketing?	performance?
production?	financing?
publicity?	management?
sales?	after sales service?

– You will soon be able to shut down!

And God said: 'At my place, it's all free! And besides, if you allow me to say so: seriously, they did some copying from me!
And at my place, not only is everything free, but the poorest are first served!...

There, I must admit, I do not make the task easy for my Church, for she lives in that world.

But I maintain her and I endorse her actions: it is free, and… I want it so: the poor are the first served. I know what I am doing'… says God.

*

So, there are some who disappear in nature, and others who meet Jesus Christ... In fact, you, the catechists, have you met Jesus Christ?

Appropriation

1. Go over your own story with Jesus Christ. Would you say that you have met him? Where? When? How?... With what results?

And there, once again, everything is said!

What you answered in the first exercise: is true... somewhat true... very true... passionately true...

Go and see your pastor and tell him where you are at. It is worth taking stock of the situation before doing catechesis. Because it is both very simple, as simple as playing a concerto on a violin, and impossible unless the violin is in the hands of a soloist.

Appropriation

2. In whose hands am I when I am with the children?

of God?	**N.B.** When you have
of Jesus Christ?	spontaneously
of the Holy Spirit?	answered this question,
of the Church?	justify your response:
of my pastor?	what concrete signs testify to it?
of the one training me?	Share with the group!

And there, once again, everything is said!
But this time, you have perceived a Church dimension,
in you, today.

Appropriation

3. Invite your pastor, share with him your journey up to this point and, with him, ask yourself:

THE CHURCH... THAT IS ALSO WHAT... STILL?

And you will say over again once more, but undoubtedly more universally, what Christian existence is all about.

Appropriation

4. Can you trace the responses, the experiences you have shared back to their origin:

EASTER – ASCENSION – PENTECOST?

What dimension does this give to your existence?

You have accepted to entrust all this to these little ones who are your brothers and sisters!

Let us give thanks to the Lord, alleluia!

6. The Christian adult – Our educative sights

The unique trait of our project for man is that it is already realized in Jesus Christ. In him, for us. Our vocation: to make him ours! On the one hand, God is first in the project. And nothing is impossible with God. On the other hand, we are limited by our own burden in the face of grace and by our density in the face of the mysterious freedom of individuals.

With such a project in our hands, we will perhaps wonder how men can say no – We ourselves say and act no: all sinners!

But since God places his trust in us, let us place ours in him: our project will become a project of faith.

To believe that we can receive ourselves as a gift of God

Renewing with the innocence that hoards nothing in its storehouses
Hoping for hope
Loving love
And taking part in this project that wants to make
sons of God with sons of men
With Jesus Christ in sight
Yesterday Today Tomorrow.

The sower went out to sow... some seeds of the Son, because God is our Father.

So, who is this Christian adult?

- The Lord alone leads him to his perfection: thus he is not complete.
- He is converted, on the way in the wake of Jesus, towards the Father.
- He knows Jesus Christ because he associates with him: he prays.
- He is on his way with his brothers and sisters, as the Church, and celebrates with them the tender love and the mercy of the Father, source of sacramental life.
- He nourishes himself from the Gospel and from the Bread of the Eucharist.
- He is capable of reading the signs of the times because he places his experience in correlation with those of Jesus Christ, of the Apostles and of the Saints.
- He is in solidarity with the pain and the joy of men, with their sin and with their redemption, he gets involved with people, for the cause of liberty and justice.
- In turn, he becomes a living centre of Revelation: through his testimony of faith, hope and charity, he invites to the Kingdom.
- He is a new man.

> When sinners are said to be justified by God, to be enlivened by the Spirit of God, to possess the life of Christ in themselves, or to have grace, we are using expressions which say the same thing in different words – that is, that they die to sin, they become sharers in the Son's divine nature through the spirit of adoption and that they enter into an intimate shared life with the Most Holy Trinity. GCD 60

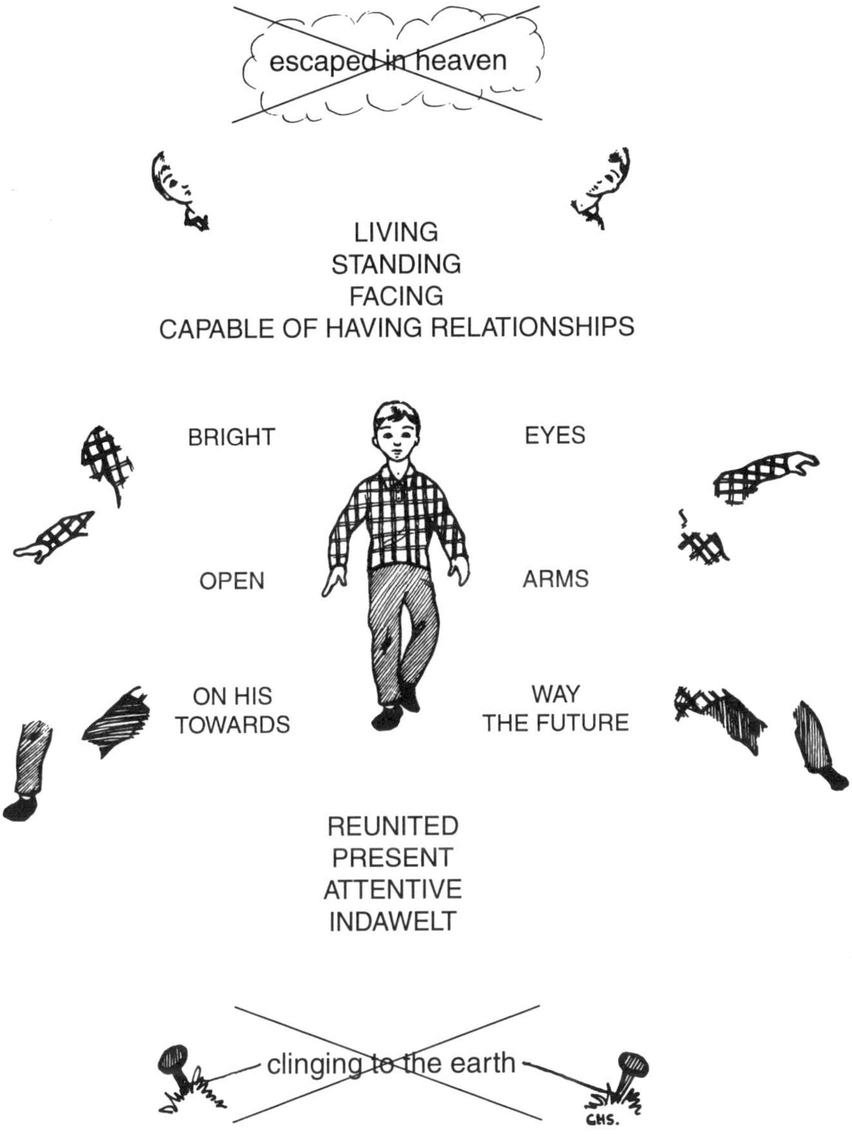

OUR EDUCATIONAL SIGHTS – THE CHRISTIAN ADULT WE ARE PREPARING

Appropriation

1. From this chapter, describe how *you* perceive the Christian adult.
2. Translate into words what the above sketch tells you.

7. The child... key to the kingdom

He called a child, whom he put among them, and said, 'Truly I tell you, unless you change and become like children, you will never enter the kingdom of heaven... Whoever welcomes one such child in my name welcomes me.' Mt 18:2-5

The little children were being brought to him in order that he might lay his hands on them and pray. The disciples spoke sternly to those who brought them; but Jesus said, 'Let the little children come to me, and do not stop them; for it is to such as these that the kingdom belongs.' And he laid his hands on them and went on his way.
Mt 19:13-15

We thought it would be a good idea to suggest that you make a little tour in the N.T., where Jesus relates children with the Kingdom, manifests a particular tenderness toward them, and, according to the sensitivities of the evangelists, blesses them, lays his hands on them, takes them up in his arms.

SOMETIMES YOU COULD BE 'JESUS' WITH THEM!...

People were bringing little children to him in order that he might touch them; and the disciples spoke sternly to them. But when Jesus saw this, he was indignant and said to them, 'Let the little children come to me; do not stop them; for it is to such as these that the kingdom of God belongs. Truly I tell you, whoever does not receive the kingdom of God as a little child will never enter it.' And he took them up in his arms, laid his hands on them, and blessed them. Mk 10:13-16

People were bringing even infants to him that he might touch them; and when the disciples saw it, they sternly ordered them not to do it. But Jesus called for them and said, 'Let the little children come to me, and do not stop them; for it is to such as these that the kingdom of God belongs. Truly I tell you, whoever does not receive the kingdom of God as a little child will never enter it.'
Lk 18:15-17

Appropriation

- Look for these texts in your Bible.
- Note the differences between the texts.
- Ask the one responsible for your formation to give you a copy of what is written in the Dictionary of Biblical Theology under the words 'CHILD' and 'KINGDOM'.
- Answer the following questions while defending your point of view:

1. Must one be a child in order to enter the Kingdom?
2. What image of the children did the disciples have?
3. By bringing these children on the scene, what does Jesus want his disciples, and us, to grasp?
4. What do Jesus' gestures make you understand?
5. Does the child symbolize a necessary attitude to have in order to accept the Kingdom? Which one?

Since we are on the subject of how we accept children and little ones, go and rejoice over the stakes in another tour:

- Mt 18:1-5; 10:40-42
- Mk 9:33-37
- Lk 9:46-48; 10:16
- Jn 13:20

"Thérèse was being asked what she understood by remaining a small child before God. She replied, 'It means that you acknowledge your own nothingness, that you expect everything from God, as a small child expects everything from its father, it means not to worry about anything, not to hoard up a fortune... To be little, moreover, is not to attribute the virtues we practise to ourselves, believing we are capable of doing things, but to acknowledge that God places this treasure in the hands of his little child, so that it may use it when need be, but it is always receiving the treasure from God.'"

Novissima Verba, 6 August 1897

Like a child = 'those who have through reflection what children have by nature'.

M. J. Lagrange

Grace and gift, the Kingdom is received as we receive a present.

8. Catechesis in the Church

We wish to confirm once more that the duty of evangelizing all men is the essential mission of the Church.

The Synod of the Bishops 1974

On the Church's identity card, it is written: 'from Jesus Christ'. The reason for her existence: being-from-Jesus-Christ-for-all-men!

The Church would die if the movement and the relationship Jesus comes to offer to all and to each on the part of his Father stopped with her.

She lives from the gospel she receives and gives... that she has received to give. The mystery of her life, her vibrant response to the Word, her prayer, her charity and her broken bread (AA 2 and ff), bear fruit when she herself becomes testimony and history.

Acceptance, gestation, openness, she brings to life:
bearer of the divine seed.

'She stands out as the sign at once mysterious and clear of the new presence of Jesus, of his setting out and of his abiding', writes Paul VI (EN 15), she prolongs and perpetuates his presence in his mission and his work.

Being apostolic by nature, she 'keeps' only to communicate with fidelity.

The purpose of the sketch on the following page is to help you become familiar with the movement of the mission of the Church.

A movement coming from far and going yet further, its culmination being the mystery of Christ: Christmas, Easter and Pentecost. Find the symbols of these in the drawing. A movement nourished by the Word and by the sacraments. A communal movement, open to everyone.

Let us recall the intensity of this mission grappling with the history of the men of today

to be evangelized
to be sanctified
to be led to the Father.

'I AM IN YOUR MIDST AS THE ONE WHO SERVES'

We think, therefore, of a Church, mystery and institution of a People of God, bearer of a creating and redeeming Word to the world, in solidarity with the poor for the promotion and liberation of everyone, in prayer to celebrate the Kingdom, seeking to make adults in faith and responsibility, having a total grasp of reality, open to dialogue and reaching out towards the future.

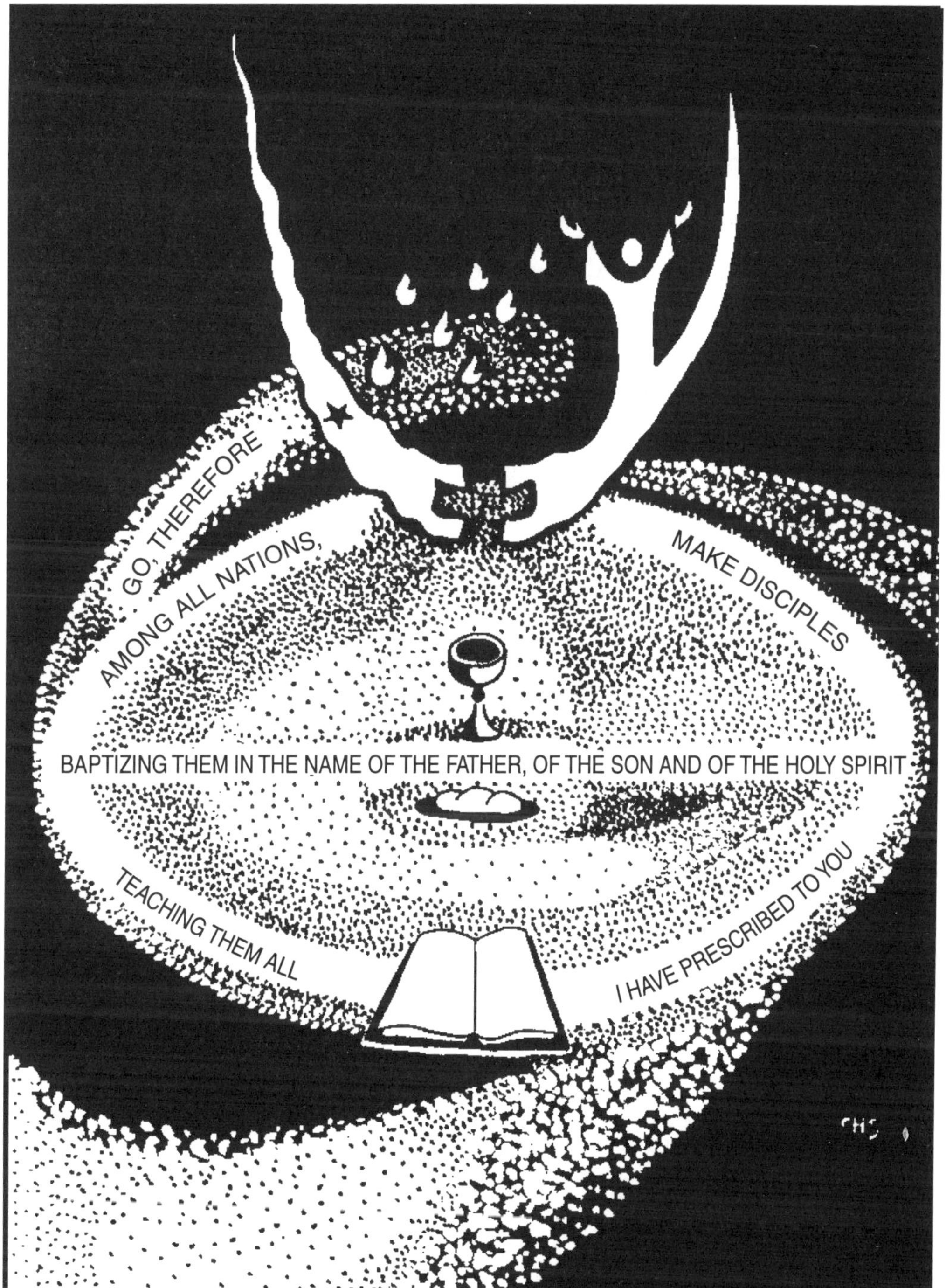
GO, THEREFORE
AMONG ALL NATIONS,
MAKE DISCIPLES
BAPTIZING THEM IN THE NAME OF THE FATHER, OF THE SON AND OF THE HOLY SPIRIT
TEACHING THEM ALL
I HAVE PRESCRIBED TO YOU

In order to assess somewhat the intensity of the Church's mission, pull out from the file 'MEDIATIONS' or 'ESSENTIAL FUNCTIONS of the Church', the card **'Kerygma'** and read its **menu**.

DEACONSHIP → Kerygma, Community, Liturgy

COMMUNITY → Deaconship, Kerygma, Liturgy

KERYGMA → Deaconship, Community, Liturgy

LITURGY → Deaconship, Kerygma, Community

Structure

Institution

Staff: see under needs

Kerygma • proclamation of the risen Christ
• first proclamation of the paschal faith
= one of the four great signs by which the Kingdom, of which the Church is a seed and a beginning, makes itself visibly present in the world.
MENU: Word – Prophecy – **Evangelization**
Catechesis – Liturgical preaching

'As the twentieth century draws to a close, the Church is bidden by God and by events – each of them a call from him – to renew her trust in catechetical activity as a prime aspect of her mission.' CT 15

'Catechesis is built on a certain number of elements of the Church's pastoral mission that have a catechetical aspect, that prepare for catechesis, or that spring from it. These elements are: the initial proclamation of the gospel or missionary preaching through the kerygma to arouse faith, apologetics or examination of the reasons for belief, experience of Christian living, celebration of the sacraments, integration into the ecclesial community, and apostolic and missionary witness.'
CT 18

The rift between the gospel and culture isundoubtedly an unhappy circumstance of our times. EN 20

Evangelization means the carrying forth of the good news to every sector of the human race so that by its strength it may enter into the hearts of men and renew the human race. 'Behold, I make all things new!' (Rev 21:5) EN 18

The gospel must be proclaimed above all else by **witness**: EN 21. **Explicit proclamation**: EN 22. **Allegiance**: EN 23.

Three remarks of capital importance for catechesis

1. 'The eternal Father chose to raise up men to share in his own divine life.' LG 2 – Not only is God extending out his hand to us, he is inviting us to his very intimacy. We are called to read into the humanity of Jesus, Son of the Father since all times, our new identity, the one effected in us by the Spirit of which Jesus was filled (cf Jn 1:1-18). Such is the dynamics of our relationship with God in faith: it brings us to the heart of God himself:

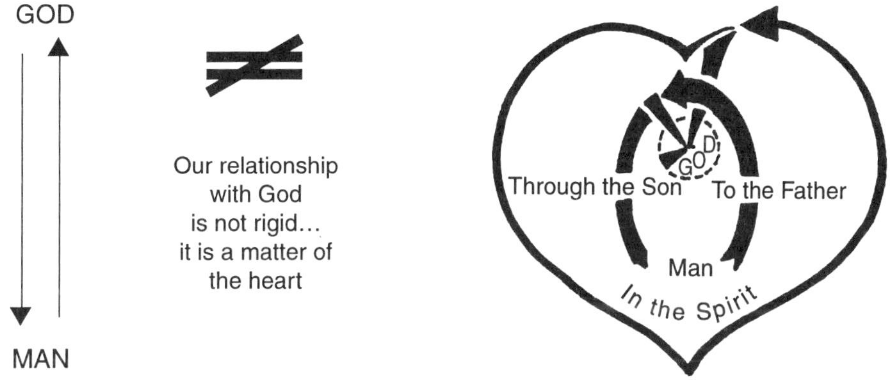

2. Jesus, the human face of God...

The Son of God, joining us in our history, manifests to us the truth of God in his humanity. He is true God and true man. But he also shows us that he covers the staggering distance between man and God. And it is because he himself has journeyed through this distance that he becomes for us the way to God.

It is on our own path that he comes to accompany us, to lead us from our present condition to future glorification!

At one stroke, Jesus reveals to us the truth about God as he realizes the truth about man. The result is a decoding to be effected which is proper to catechesis. God speaks 'man' in the Revelation and in his Son. The Holy Spirit enables us to speak 'God' in faith. The correlation will help us to decode this (chapter 28).

3. Finally, catechists, you have a part to play in the mission of the Church. In the revealing movement of the mystery of God, you are sacrament. So, pray your encounters before engaging yourselves on your way. Thus you will make the transparent image of a life of relationship and of communion within the reach of the hearts of the children.

Appropriation

For each of the three 'remarks of capital importance', complete the following sentence: 'In concrete terms, it means that...'

9. Can we transmit faith?

And how are they to believe in one of whom they have never heard? And how are they to hear without someone to proclaim him? Rom 10:14

Faith is something so intimate and personal that we cannot 'pass' it on like an object bequeathed to one's heirs.

That is true. And yet, we are forced to acknowledge that for two thousand years, there has well and truly existed a transmission of faith. But it does not have the automatic trait of a legacy, it is not the fruit of training or of a simple process of learning. What, therefore, is the meaning of 'transmitting the faith'?

The definitive aim of catechesis is to put people not only in touch but in communion, in intimacy, with Jesus Christ (John Paul II, CT 5).

FAITH is the free acceptance of this communion with Christ. That cannot be imposed from the outside. And yet, says John Paul II, CATECHESIS can and must aim at eliciting and realizing this free and personal experience. The document, on the following page, may help us to understand what this is about.

Faith, when all is said and done, is transmitted somewhat like the incentive to live and love: through a close relationship of trust, through patterns of behaviour that witness to life and love, through words conveying its profound meaning.

Faith is what God alone can give in the most intimate experience of each. But, in the hands of those who have received it, this gift of God becomes a richness to share and pass on, in humility and with a sense of responsibility.

Appropriation

1. Take time to read and meditate on the text on the next page. Let it echo in you. Then, do the 'counter-test': imagine a catechesis in which one of the four elements emphasized were missing... would this be serious? Why?...
2. For which of the four elements do you feel better prepared or more able? Which one is for you a call to progress? How can you foster and take charge of this progress?
3. Recall your own journey in faith. What were its outstanding stages? Who helped you, supported you? How? Do you rediscover one or several of the four elements? How did they 'interplay' with one another in your life?
4. How did Jesus 'transmit' his faith? For instance, read over Luke 4 and 5; 19:1-10; 24:13-35. Note what is most striking to you.
5. In the manner of 'transmitting', what do you see that is the same or different in what can be done: in parish catechesis? in the family? at school? in daily life, in the chain of events and encounters?

❶ There is something
– someone! –
to TELL

❷ Not just anything
– not just anyone! –
REVELATION
– the revealer! –

Learning to communicate

To set about to listen to and learn from Revelation

The Lord has sent us to evangelize men. But have you given thought to what evangelizing men means?

Evangelizing a man, you see, is to tell him: You, too, are loved by God in the Lord Jesus. And not only telling him that, but really thinking it.

And not only thinking it, but acting with this man in such a way that he will feel and discover that there is something saved in him, something greater and nobler than he thought, and that he is thus awakened to a new awareness of self. That is what proclaiming the Good News to him means. You cannot do so except by offering him your friendship. A true friendship, disinterested without condescension, made of profound trust and esteem.

E. Leclerc, Sagesse d'un pauvre.
Franciscan ed.

Interiorizing, converting one's heart, praying

Acting in truth, reaching out to love

❸ Saying nothing
that is not
ROOTED
IN THE HEART

❹ ACTIONS AND
RELATIONSHIPS
speak louder
than words!

10. Bible and symbol source of catechesis

When God reveals himself he leaves us his address.
We know he is there wherever he comes.
He comes
in his **Word**
in his Son made **man**
in the **Church** which transmits it.

Indeed, born of the Word, the Church gives it a body, lives from it, adopts it and brings it to life in the world of history: that is what we call the living Tradition of the Church.[1]

By passing on the Bible to men – not as a book, but as the Word of God – she is offering the original faith, the one which adopted the very expression of the writings of the New Testament. These already contain the first catecheses of the history of the Church!

Now, a specific fruit of catechesis is to express the acceptance of the Word of God as a profession of faith.

That is how the 'CREDO' or the 'CREED OF FAITH' plays a special role in this living tradition as a synthesis of the expression of faith. The Apostles' Creed, besides, was handed to the catechumens with the 'Our Father' in the course of a celebration so that they could 'give it back' at their baptismal profession.

While re-reading the boxed-in texts of this page, note how the living and acting Word of God is light for life, how a life of faith makes our story a history of salvation and how, in turn, the Church becomes a sign of the Gospel and a call to conversion.

1. Inasmuch as it is a founding source, Tradition, along with the Scriptures, is fulfilled in the time of the Apostles. It extends itself, as a living deployment, throughout the whole history of the Church (cf also drawing p. 33).

'There is no true evangelization if the name, the teaching, the life, the promises, the kingdom and the mystery of Jesus of Nazareth, the Son of God, are not proclaimed. 'The whole history of the Church, beginning with the sermon of Peter on the day of Pentecost, is interwoven and united with the history of this proclamation.' EN 22 'For evangelization will never achieve its full force and significance unless it is received, accepted and adopted, and unless it evokes the wholehearted allegiance of those who hear it. A man may assent to the truths which a merciful God has revealed, but he will give a much deeper and fuller assent to the spirit and way of life – that is a life now transformed – which those truths propose to him. (...) This allegiance, which cannot detract from the external circumstances of life, is expressed by the visible and objective entry of a man into the community of the faithful.' EN 23

'Authentic catechesis is always an orderly and systematic initiation into the revelation that God has given of himself to humanity in Christ Jesus, a revelation stored in the depths of the Church's memory and in Sacred Scripture, and constantly communicated from one generation to the next by a living active traditio. This revelation is not however isolated from life or artificially juxtaposed to it. It is concerned with the ultimate meaning of life and it illumines the whole life with the light of the Gospel, to inspire it or to question it.' CT 28

Let us conclude with John Paul II: 'To speak of Tradition and Scripture as the source of catechesis is to draw attention to the fact that catechesis must be impregnated and penetrated by the thought, the spirit and the outlook of the Bible and the Gospels through assiduous contact with the texts themselves; but it is also a reminder that catechesis will be all the richer and more effective for reading the texts with the intelligence and the heart of the Church and for drawing inspiration from the two thousand years of the Church's reflection and life.' CT 27

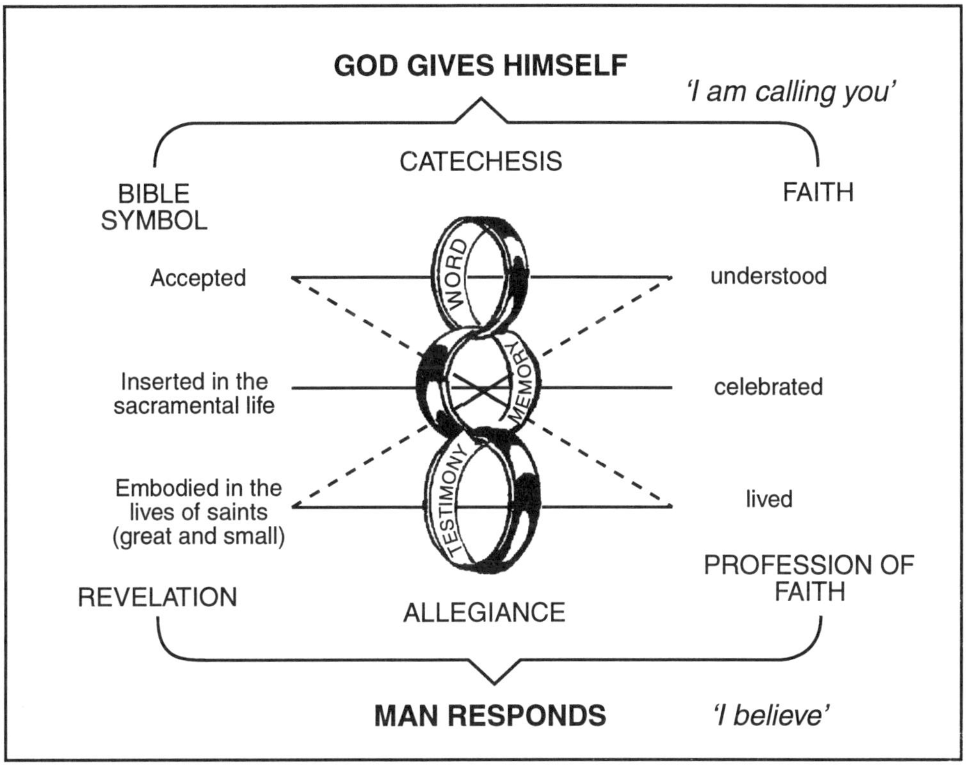

Appropriation

1. There are six pages (42-48) to read on the 'hows' underlined on the previous page in the reference text of the French Episcopal Conference: *La Catéchèse des enfants*, 1979. This exercise is necessary to deepen the 'functioning' of Revelation which is effected as distance, as call, and as way. This is interesting because it opens the field to the process of correlation!

2. Discuss, among yourselves, about the horizontal, diagonal and vertical significance of the sketch on this page, in order to place your ministry within the constellation

Word – Life – Faith.

11. The guiding documents of catechesis

- Documents of the Second Vatican Council
- General Catechetical Directory (GCD)
- Paul VI, Evangelization in the Modern World (EN)
- John Paul II, Catechesis in our time (CT)

As an initiative and a gift of God, faith opens a working site where the believer develops his answers, grows, matures, commits himself to and for the Kingdom of God. The Church accompanies him on his journey, better yet... she grows in him and he in her: 'Changed by the working of grace into a new creature, the Christian thus sets himself to follow Christ and learns more and more within the Church to think like him, to judge like him, to act in conformity with his commandments, and to hope as he invites us to.' John Paul II, CT 20.

DEFINITION

'Catechesis is an education of children, young people and adults in the faith, which includes especially the teaching of Christian doctrine imparted, generally speaking, in an organic and systematic way, with a view to initiating the hearers into the fullness of Christian life.' CT 18, cf 21.

What if the first evangelization has not taken place? cf CT 19

?

AIM

"To put it more precisely: within the whole process of evangelization, the aim of catechesis is to be the teaching and maturation stage, that is to say, the period in which the Christian, having accepted by faith the person of Jesus Christ as the one Lord and having given him complete adherence by sincere conversion of heart, endeavours to know better this Jesus to whom he has intrusted himself: to know his 'mystery', the Kingdom of God proclaimed by him, the requirements and promises contained in his Gospel message, and the paths that he has laid down for anyone who wishes to follow him." CT 20, cf GCD 38-39

CONTENT

= **that of the entire evangelization**

'The one message – the Good News of salvation – that has been heard once or hundreds of times and has been accepted with the heart, is in catechesis probed unceasingly by reflection and systematic study, by awareness of its repercussions on one's personal life – an awareness calling for ever greater commitment – and by inserting into it an organic and harmonious whole, namely Christian living in society and the world.' CT 26, cf GCD 39, 45 EN 25 - 39; 44

- Integrity CT 30 GCD 37, 39-44
- Where method and language remain instruments CT 31
- Ecumenical, 32
- limited collaboration 33
- **Principal elements of the Christian mystery** GCD 7-69

TASKS

– Bring about and foster conversion CT 19

– Lead to a full knowledge of the mystery of Christ CT 20, 27, 28, 30 GCD 24, 38, 43

Principal elements

– Initiate into the commitment in CT 23, 24 GCD 22-31

of the Christian the Church and in the world mystery GCD 47-69

– Elicit and bring the interior attitudes of a life of faith to maturity.

'Whatever you say, do so in a way that the one to whom you are speaking may believe by listening to you, may hope by believing, may love by hoping.'

St Augustine, *La catéchèse des débutants*

BENEFICIARIES

Everyone	–	Small children	CT 36	GCD 78	
EN 49-58	–	Children	37	79-81	
	–	Adolescents	38	82-90	
	–	Young people	39-40, 42		
	–	Handicapped	41	91	
	–	Adults	43-44	92-97	
	–	In diversified and complementary catecheses			CT 45
The whole man	–	'man's innermost being'			CT 52
	–	and bring the power of the Gospel into the very heart of culture and cultures			CT 53

METHOD

An original pedagogy of the faith	CT 58	GCD 33, 46	
An adapted language	59	34 –>	EN 62-64
EN ch. II, especially 21-23	GCD 35		

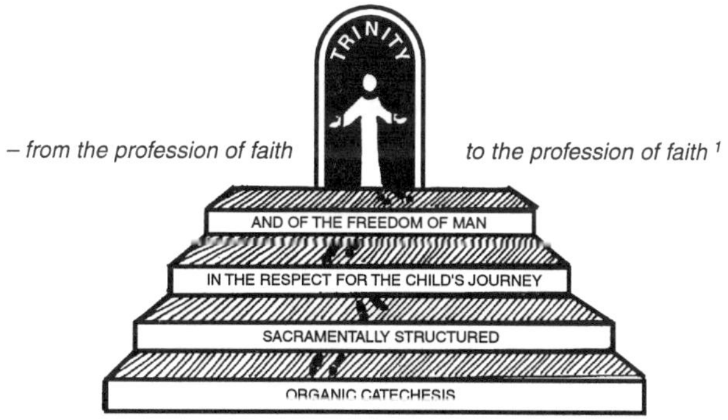

[1] *Address to the people of God (No 8)*

Appropriation

Get one of the quoted documents (GCD, EN or CT) and take half an hour to acquaint yourself with its content. Share your impressions with the group.

12. The catechetical initiative

Garage ways

Catechesis...

– Communication of religious facts: a doctrine to memorize	... as if God wanted to exercise our memory
– Reflection on some current problems	... as if God were revealing that men ought to be intelligent
– Application of the religious message on the practical aspects of life	... as if God were giving out recipes on how to become religious
– Juxtaposition of the Christian message and situations allowing it to 'pass on'	... as if God wanted to give us a dictation on our lives.

All that is not entirely false.

For some of us, having had a taste of it did not make us die! Nevertheless, the essential initiative we deal with is missing.

THE WHOLE STAKES CONSIST OF THIS

God is the one who takes the initiative of communicating himself. IMMANOU-EL, God-with-us: nothing that is human is alien to him.

Our life is not a simple site of practice, but the very place for Revelation to take place. God is already there, present in our history, because he cares infinitely for us. It is up to us to make of our present a presence in his PRESENCE. To limit ourselves to 'pass on' the message is to remain outside the movement of Revelation.

> 'Catechesis is the constant attempt – adapted to the various ages of man – to identify, within a group of persons well-disposed toward the faith, the unknown God in their lives, as the God who revealed himself in the Bible, in the history of the people of Israel and, in an unparalleled way, in Jesus of Nazareth, to renew their own faith in this way, without confusing it neither with the collective credulity nor with the individualistic religiosity.'
>
> G. Bauder, quoted by E. Alberich, *La Catéchèse dans l'Eglise,* p. 100.

Thus, it is always the Father who, in his Son
Jesus Christ, takes the route of man
to overtake a man,
a community,
his people.
In catechesis,
we always act
upon the initiative of an Other.
It is always the ecclesial Community
that sends us, in the Name of Jesus Christ, the Lord.

As a catechist, I have an experience of Jesus Christ, as Church. Thus, I have deepened my experience of faith, I have confronted it with that of my Church – sometimes, not without pain – but I have identified my experience with those, the founding ones, of Jesus and the Apostles (cf chapter 14).

I hold what Jesus said and did to be true... what the Apostles have transmitted to us. I believe with them and as they did.

What was valid for them, is valid for me.

I am in communion with them in a common faith; this gift God makes in us of his Spirit. There lies the most profound and vital truth that comes to me and dwells in me: I have begun to see, to hear, to think, to speak and to live as Jesus does. I rediscover in myself the IMAGE from which I am 'stamped'.

With my brothers and sisters, the little ones of the catechism, the grown-ups with whom I share my journey, I am ready to re-read their lives and mine, their story and mine, in the light of the Word of God.

At the same time, there is the Word of God which has taken flesh in me, it informs my life and allows me to witness. That made St Paul say, 'It is no longer I who live, but it is Christ who lives in me!' (Gal 2:20).

Indeed, all this is not linear in our story: we go through our growth crises, and then, we cannot persevere in fidelity in this world without the cross beckoning to us. It, too, stretches out its arms towards the Word of the Lord.

Before making a schematic drawing of the catechetical initiative, it has appeared absolutely necessary to suggest the intimate work which underpins the profession of faith and to measure to some extent the depth of its roots.

That, besides, helps us to respect the journeys of our searching brothers and sisters in catechesis. There is no question here of buttering up or of applying a coat of Catholic paint, but of creating the conditions of a first experience of faith in the children who come to us without any evangelization and of accompanying the other children by using a pedagogy that reaches them.

The catechetical initiative is not made outside history. On the contrary, it proclaims the salvation offered at the very heart of all human history. It seizes history in order to reveal its meaning and its stakes.

The catechetical initiative

FROM A FAITH SEARCHING FOR ITSELF

according to Luke 24:13-35

1 *Overtaking* ➤
... wherever they live
get in touch
invitation

2 *Welcoming* ➤
Open a material,
relational
space, where they
can be themselves

In Church: create bonds

5 *Giving THE WORD* ➤
Search
in the light of Scripture
of the faith experience of the
Church
a Word which
challenges
nourishes
invites

6 *Giving one's own presence* ➤
Allowing
oneself
to become involved
inviting
welcoming

Was it not necessary
Christ should suffer these things
and then enter into his glory?...
He explained to them
the things about himself
in all the Scriptures.

Stay with us
... So
he went in
to stay
with them.

Appropriation

Take this plan as a reading guide for your habitual use. Did you experience anything of this initiative during the recent months? Make your answer concrete by giving examples.

TO A FAITH THAT IS FOUND AS CHURCH AND THAT WITNESSES

3 *Asking* ➤
the right questions
aiming at the experiences
which lead to the
experience
of faith

4 *Letting others speak (= listening)* ➤
eliciting, fostering expression
Children alone can say
who they are
where they are at

establish communication – in communion

7 *Celebrating* ➤
a growth
in meaning
a superabundance
of PRESENCE

8 *Re-reading* ➤
the distance covered
communicating to one another
the experience
of faith

9 *Sending* ➤
to spread
and share
the news:
He is alive

A NEW LOOK

A RENEWED LIFE

He took bread
blessed and
broke it,
and gave it
to them.

Were not our hearts
burning
within us
while he was
talking to us
on the road
and reading the Scriptures to us?

They left
and told
what had happened
on the way.

13. Parents and catechists

The family remains, along with the parents and the grandparents, the setting for the first awakenings to life of the child: the ears, the eyes, and language. The space for the first gestures and the first steps. The polarization of the first relationships. The milieu that leaves its mark. Briefly: the hearth of the first experiences! Man is history...

Hearing this, for catechists, amounts to a mobilization: it is everything that was brought to life, there, that they will have to deal with in catechesis.

You are familiar with the pictures of Jesus and the Church that come to you with the children. You also know thc desert, and the hunger that some children come to ask you to nourish.

Because of your mandate, you are thus called to be in touch with the families of the children of catechesis, either with the parents or with those who take their place in this role.

– First because you are their partners in the education of the children.

– Then, because your relationship with them establishes an atmosphere of esteem and clarity.

– Finally, because you will put them in relation with their community, in a way different from that of the pastor.

> 'The economy of salvation is being perfected in the temporal order. It began in the past, progressed towards its apex in Christ, unfolds its meaning in the present time and awaits its completion in the future.' GCD 44

> The Community already there represents the first milieu of reference for the initiation into the Church. The choice of a strategy of evangelization of the homes indifferent to faith is to be made then and there, as a group, with the one responsible for pastoral work.

You will thus set up a network of relationships which will bear fruit in all the future interventions: parent meetings, preparation for the sacraments, celebrations and the intense moments of life in the community. And above all, when we know the tree!...

We urge you to read chapter 29 which deals directly with the parents.

In this chapter, we suggest that you reflect in a practical way on parents meetings. As a catechist, you will have to organize such meetings. They are privileged opportunities not only to make contacts but to evangelize: it is up to you to reveal to the parents what they are often living already without being clearly conscious of doing so. The guidelines that follow do not offer you 'devices or tricks' but suggest a spirit your meetings could have.

On parents' meetings

A conviction dwells in us. It is called gift, mercy, inspiration, 'beginning' written 'as if sowing',[1] as well as coherence.

Imagine this: you are preparing a fire, twigs, small branches, larger ones, carefully stacked up in the shape of a pyramid... the wood supply is ready...

No matches!

Yes, it is somewhat like that: it is a matter, not of inducing the ecstasy, but of setting on fire! What precisely gives spirit to a technique, some soul to a method? What transforms a cry into a call, a gesture into an embrace, a word into a saying, a message into a gospel? Someone behind, or under, and we find ourselves face to face with a presence.

There are tricks which work: flash-in-the-pan fires we watch. We meet people. They do not do things, they are simply there. And because they are there, their mediation makes you forget them. You are the one who comes, who comes out of a shell, sometimes even out of a fortress. They have liberated you from your fears, and perhaps from the dizzying effects of the sin. Jesus must have been like that...

A PARENTS' MEETING IS A RENDEZVOUS

'What shall I say to them?', 'In any case, that is of no interest to them', 'They are like fossils!'

There, the problem lies in you. Not in them. Do not be mistaken about that!

They have a day's work behind them; they have one or more children; marital, family, school, social problems; their heart is full of knots and questions; they are in a mixed marriage situation, perhaps remarried; they are 'centred on their own thing' or are alienated, labourer or middle-class; they have an image of God and the Church, sometimes a shocking one. Whatever that may be, you are dealing not with the 'lost' people but with the 'saved'. Here is how you can give them a foretaste of this in the meeting.

1. The meeting has already begun with the **invitation**:

Dear parents,

You, first, are the ones responsible for the religious education of your children as the Second Vatican Council has affirmed.

or:

It is a pleasure for me, dear parents, to know that soon we shall discuss together about the growth happening in the hearts of your children... So...

For a certain number of parents, this written invitation is the first contact with you, with the Christian community. A paper contact, to be sure, but possibly a decisive one. They will come or they will not come, in a particular state of mind, according to what they will have read and seen in the invitation. Write your messages carefully!

1. The last words of Pierre Moitel in his book: *Je crois... Comment le dire*? Centurion 1983.

2. Before the meeting, in order to find your place again at the heart of your ministry, pray:

– *Lord, as small... as tiny... as I may feel. Before you and before what is awaiting me this evening: meeting men, women whom I know so little, whom you know so well. What would you tell them?*

– *Create the means for me to tell them that I love you. Without words, with your smile, your difficulties. It is always the same: they must recognize themselves in what you say!*

– *You believe?*
– *And you?*
– *You are, indeed, always the same!*
– *You see: you recognize me!*
– *Lord...*
– *Go now and prepare the agenda of the meeting!*
– ...
– *Yes, go!*

3. They arrive. You wrote to them: with joy. Show them the truth of this in the *welcome* you give them. And give to some the task of welcoming others, especially if you know them already.

The tables and chairs must be set in such a way as to promote communication.

4. The most important point is that they experience the fact that they are reached and that their real life is taken into account!

They bear within themselves for their children a source of life and devotion greater than the one you will ever manage to reach, even if they have a poor way of manifesting their love. You have a keen sense of this if you yourself are a father or a mother. Join them on the path of their personal history.

At first, they might try to test you, to check what you really stand for. Transfer those questions to the group to detect your allies and monitor the patterns or relationships taking form among the parents. In fact, your meeting cannot be reduced to a discussion with one couple: the others would no longer be reached. In a word:

reach them,
so that they may recognize themselves in what you are saying
and find themselves again in what you are suggesting.

This is a learning process? – Yes.

But, first, a way of being and acting which is translated into a manner of approach, a language, a presence!... Your evaluations will be a help to you!

5. Fraternal? – Must this be mentioned? – No, you must be so! Because it is true: 'You are all brothers'.

This implies some checking at the time of the preparation of the meeting: what do I say, what do I do, what do I prepare, what place do I give to the RELATIONAL aspect? Who is meeting whom? Concerning what relationship? What experience of relationship or rejection? The objects, the events, among whom do they establish communication?

If you could announce at the end of a meeting: 'Did you notice? We spoke about man during the whole evening: man as he is set in relation to others, as he takes risks, seeks a place among others, opens up or is hurt because of others... that is our everyday life. And our little ones grow up amidst all that! You, the parents, have already gone through much with them! From where does the idea come that you are ready for anything for their sake?... There, we have touched God's great project!'

6. For not a single instant must the parents think they are at school. But with them, put yourself at the Master's 'school', humble and filial.

Let your attitude suggest the presence of an Other. Also use a language that suits the One the parents already know or seek!

Perhaps not so much like this:	*as in this way:*
'I am not the one saying this, God is.'	'That happens to you as it does to me, I am sure, that you feel totally renewed because of a glance, a word, an encounter... It is as if we were coming out of our shell, like a liberation. You have noticed: at those moments, even if we do not have faith, we think of God.'

7. You know that we should not turn the knife in a wound. Parents have antennae, just touch them: a hedgehog all bristled up! We would readily say that they will sit at your table if they have discovered that you speak up for them.

8. People complain everywhere. They did not come to listen to lamentations, but to know the person to whom they have entrusted their children. You are playing higher stakes than it would appear. You symbolize a ray of hope for the parents!

9. The concern to give a brilliant impression, which fascinates us all, is a pitfall to avoid: the parents are the ones who must shine, without any flattery or concessions. Harmony among them, between them and you, is already, in a budding stage, an experience of Church.

Acknowledge their place as something you need in order to hold your own.

Meeting together, drawing up the programme as a group, tracing the course, outlining the objectives, will stimulate their participation.

Deciding together about what contributes to the education of their children is the best way of mobilizing their sense of responsibility.

10. Finally, with the glass of friendship 'celebrating' your meeting, bring it to an early close!... Not because of fatigue but because you cannot negotiate the stakes of their children's education in faith in one evening:

- either it is sold off at a cheap price and they made a mistake in coming to the sales;
- or they realize this is serious and they are ready to come again.

Let them express themselves, so that they themselves may suggest to you to have another meeting!

You will sow: they will reap

The ten commandments of the catechist in a meeting

1. YOU SHALL INVITE THEM: they will feel called
2. YOU SHALL PRAY YOUR MEETING: they will people your offering
3. YOU SHALL WELCOME THEM: they will feel at home
4. YOU SHALL REACH THEM: they will give you of their lives
5. YOU SHALL BE BROTHER: they will have a glimpse of their Father
6. YOU SHALL NOT "KNOW": they will be happy to search with you
7. YOU SHALL NOT PROVOKE THEM: they will tell you their hurts
8. YOU SHALL NOT COMPLAIN: they will invite you
9. YOU SHALL NOT SHINE: they will play the role of partners
10. YOU SHALL NOT BE LENGTHY: they will still be hungry.

Appropriation

1. Starting from guidelines in this chapter and from your experience, build up as a team a little (or a large) memory jogger to make your meetings with the parents a success.
2. Read chapter 29 and answer the following: In your personal encounters, in meetings with parents, are you concerned about giving importance to the irreplaceable role of the parents and family experiences? Do you give them the opportunity to express themselves? How could it be done better or more be done? Make a concrete decision to be realized in the near future and determine its procedure (What? When? Where? How?)...
3. Make the counter-test: for each of our commandments, imagine the errors, the opposite attitudes. In your opinion, what are the consequences of these?

14. Catechists with others

How are they to call on one in whom they have not believed? And how are they to believe in one of whom they have never heard? And how are they to hear without someone to proclaim him ... unless they are sent? Rom 10:14-15

A large ecclesial body, the MINISTRY of the WORD

- assuring the mission of the Church in a twofold fidelity
  – to the teaching Christ
  – to the beneficiaries of all nations

- involving all her missionaries in their personal life

- including the catechist of a small village who has received the mandate from the pastor, to the magisterium of the bishops and the pope, but first of all the entire Church in a commanded service: 'All power has been given me in heaven and in earth, go forth!...'

'The evangelizers' (EN chapter VI) are supported by the same groups as 'those responsible for catechesis' (CT chapter IX), and with good reason! Their respective roles appear to us to be adequately described in these reference texts.

You wish to know, for example, how the bishops and the priests ought to follow the spirit and the norms of Vatican II?...

– Go and read the 'Decree on the pastoral office of bishops in the Church' and the 'Decree on the ministry and life of priests', or yet again the new Canon Law.

The audacity of a mission

'Courage, hope and enthusiasm', writes John Paul II to those who are in charge of catechesis and 'training for a life in keeping with the Gospel'! (CT 62)

– 'I am trained...' 'I go to be trained...' They well know what they are talking about, the children of catechism!

– And so do we!

By coming to catechesis, they will say someday, 'I go to be trained for Life. We have mass on Sunday, we are on the side of Jesus Christ. Last Sunday, we won against hunger; this week is against lying. And then, soon, we shall take part in the Paschal tournament... we are a little afraid: it is against death. But we have a trainer who works like that!'

That things be thus depends on them, on their milieu, on the world wrangling over them; but that also depends on us.

And there, catechists, priests, bishops, the pope, we know for a fact that, first, there is no question of organization or method, but of faith and love, and therefore, for all of us, a question of training!

Now, we are allowed to enter into the gratuitousness of God. Not for what it can bring to us but for what it means, 'what it produces, what it creates.' 'Come the day when we will not be burning with love,' Mauriac used to say, 'many men will die of cold.'

Whatever the nature of the call you heard to enter into the catechetical ministry, this textbook offers you a survey of yourpractical work. Its value depends on your training, already completed, to begin or to pursue.

However, your training needs to draw upon the gratuitouscharacter of the Source!

You received without payment; give without payment (Mt 10:8)

We firmly believe that the secret of catechesis is to actualize God's way of giving himself, through pure initiative, creating a space, a volume for men in which they can freely structure their response.

There are always people who tug at the petals of flowers to make them grow faster. As for yourselves, allow the children some time for their spiritual growth – the first initiative for a number of them – offer them the human space they need to raise themselves towards God.

You will be like the Source if you believe that 'the strength by which you love them is no different from the one by which they exist.' (Claudel)

Forming a team

Transmitting faith! If it is possible to teach religion without believing in God, on the other hand, it is impossible to transmit faith (cf chapter 9) without expressing my experience of the Word of God and without referring to its centre and summit, Jesus Christ in person (chapter 8). But where can we find him 'in person' if not in these persons who, with me, are the Church?

In catechesis, we cannot be a 'small independent contractor' and a solitary one! Catechesis aims at building the Church, at assembling in unity. This fruit can mature only on the community roots. As catechists, we lead to the community inasmuch as we are part of the community. How can we speak of the Church if we do not live its reality? Besides, we know very well from experience how our teams of work and sharing are indispensable places of renewal, of verification, of joy. For lack of a team and sharing, some catechists lose heart after a few years and they are out of breath. Others, on the contrary, renew themselves and last without wearing themselves out thanks to the team of which they are a member.

You are not far...

You are not far from
the Kingdom...

Keep on going, for what
limit could you assign
to the unique love
which has captivated you?
You will never come to
the end of your human
route on my divine route.
You will never come to
the end of encountering
in your richness a
disarming poverty.

You will never come to the
end of your human route
on my divine route.
You will never come to the
end of purifying your rites
from all idols and from all
harshness.

You will never come to the
end of your human route
on my divine route.
You will never finish
making your prayer sing
to the sound of your justice.

You will never come to the
end of your human route
on my divine route.
You will never finish
breaking down your
certitudes to be born
to the truth.
Keep on going
for Yahweh your God
is the God of your search
of your call, of your desire.

Excerpt from *Manuel de catéchèse pour jeunes et adultes* by André Fossion, p.330, Desclée 1985.

Also, the formation of catechists is effected within a group which makes itself Church, where each one opens up to the others, communicates with them, takes the risk of interpreting his experience, challenges and lets himself be challenged, bears and is borne, checks and makes himself acknowledged.

We are at the heart of the relational!

And it is in this process that faith is expressed and given. That you are not far from is where we mature in faith, and the Kingdom... are led from within to celebrate the truth and goodness of God in Jesus Christ.

> It is because my experience of God is always confronted against and referred to that of my Church, that I can 'take risks' in his name.

Whether the group starts off from an experience of life, to place it in correlation with the founding experience of Jesus and the Apostles (biblical accounts), or whether it follows the opposite road, it matters little!

From the moment a dialogue is established between the founding experience and the actual experience, these are confronted and re-examined: they become a place of revelation and proposition of faith:

- God expresses his presence to me...
- I meet Jesus the Saviour...
- I find myself loved... liberated... saved...

The source of the celebration is already there. It springs forth in thanksgiving: our existence is transfigured, our humanity visited, our person indwelt.

We recognize the Lord: he hears us, forgives us, shares his life with us and... sends us!

Basically, we become catechists, through the initiative we take ourselves, as Church.

So then?

– Lord, if you want to accomplish anything with me... here I am!... here we are!...

...The 'risk'? It is to fathom something of the depth of the baptism which has opened to us, in the Church, the road to the Eucharist, to the sacraments and to an inexhaustible spiritual vitality!

At the crossroads of relationships

To conclude, we are making a stop on your being-in-the-world as a catechist, for you are at a crossroads of relationships which constitute the web into which you weave in your intervention.

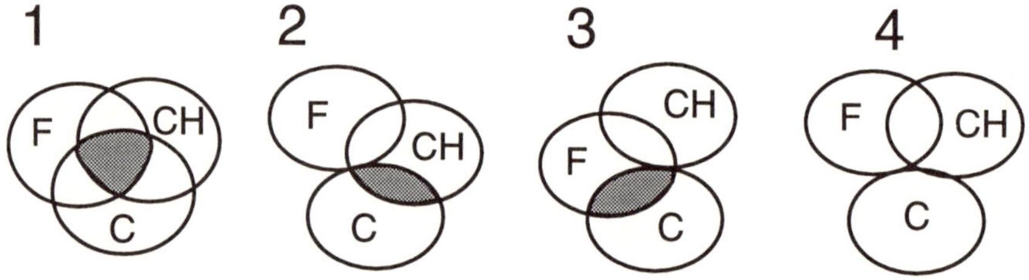

F = FAMILY C = COMMUNITY CH = CHILD

The children you meet, in practical terms, can be found in four situations.

As a catechist, you believe that the Holy Spirit carries you in your ecclesial mandate, and that he is at work in the heart of your children.

You know, that because of their situation, you cannot intervene in an unequivocal way or put the children through a rolling mill: they each have their autonomy.

You are doing what?

– I am giving up!
– No! you re-read the page!

The group of catechists and the one responsible for it

The local Community and the priest responsible for it

The Council of evangelization

The school, as the case may be

The parish groupings of children

To be sure this is not easy, otherwise you would not be there! The children and their group go around to the persons concerned with the pastoral situation:

So many persons and institutions who, because of their responsibility, find themselves faced with the same problem as you are...

and so many resources and so many complementarities in the evangelization movement which mobilizes the Church of today: you are not alone!

You are playing the role of an antenna: transmitting the message! The credibility of the Church in your own eyes is at stake.

It is therefore a matter of identifying your first area of negotiation.

In order to authenticate the ecclesial dimension you bear in your ministry: share, be Church, with the other members of the same body; and commit yourselves with them in the strategy of welcome and companionship with the littles ones, wherever they are, as they are, to lead them to Jesus Christ, wherever he comes.

We insist on this type of pastoral arrangement. It is a constituent of your ministry.

There are, in fact, some elements of coherence we must create in our communities. And you would not want to be, for all that, at work in the ministry of the Word of God without having the right to speak in your own Church! God spoke in order to give his Word.

Without any doubt, there is some polishing to do sometimes – a question of training – but it opens out to a discovery we all make as we grow in experience: layers of congenital misery tied to our human condition, and underlying it... hearts that hide, that do not speak, that have been silenced, who will even seem to stiffen at your approach, but who are all waiting for the Church, because they have been tailored according to God's expectations!

... suppose a sole one would start to speak because of you...

"That is why we can apply to catechists an expression used by the Second Vatican Council with special reference to priests: 'instructors (of the human being and his life) in the faith'." CT 22

Appropriation

1. Are you a member of a team of which you can say: for me it is a place of training? If so, express your gratitude to one another as a team! If not, who could help you form a team?
2. What is, or are, for you the concrete place(s) of communion and negotiation where you can share your experiences as a catechist with others responsible for the community?

15. The role of the priest

Keep watch over yourselves and over all the flock.
Acts 20:28

Theoretically, everything is simple. The priest is the first catechist of his community. He is also answerable for what others do along with him. He is the living sign of the bond with the bishop and with the ecclesial communion. But in practical terms, the situations are complex and varied.

Bernard, pastor of a large village

Bernard, you are doing the catechesis in your parish. That is your choice. You even refused the help of a person from the outside who was offering to assist you. Why?

Indeed, this is a choice I made. The explanation is simple. The population of this village forms a human community enjoying cohesion and stability. Not that the people here are better than in the city, but they have a collective identity and their roots are in the parish. They all know each other, there are many bonds.

What relation is there with your choice of assuring the catechesis of the children yourself?

Of course, through the children I reach the whole community. What I do with them has an enormous repercussion on the parents, on the families. Knowing all the children personally, having a good relationship with them, I have a link with the families. At the time of the sacramental stages, especially, but also in an ongoing way. The parents are aware that I know their son, their daughter. When I meet them, we speak of the children and they are interested. If I visit a family, I am all the more welcome because the children love me and I love them.

In short, far from distancing the adults, the children bring you closer to them?

Exactly. Sometimes we oppose the catechesis of the little ones against the catechesis of the adults, as if we had less to do for the first and more for the second. For me, here, that is not at all the case. The children open up the door of the parents to me. This is not the only door, to be sure, but it is one that counts. Moreover, starting from the children, I can build up the unity of the community, were it but at the level of liturgy: the hymns or the prayers learnt in catechesis are accepted by the parents at home and they find them again in church. It is the same for other aspects: the spirit and orientation for the time of Lent or Advent, for example.

And the future? In ten years, perhaps there will no longer be a priest in your parish?

That is true. But this is an overall problem touching all our sector, of pastoral work. It is within the framework of this sector that we prepare for the future: by reflecting in a global perspective, by inviting laypersons to be trained... This work in this sector is of capital importance. It is also important that structures of formation exist.

Peter, in an urban parish

Peter, you are experiencing a very different reality...

Yes, in the city, the human fabric is scattered. There is great mobility. The face of the collectivity changes constantly. The proportion of 'religious practice' is low, about 10%. There can be no question of this link between the children and the community, as described by Bernard.

And the priests, I imagine, are torn between the many urgent demands!

Indeed! I could never take on the catechesis of all the children. And even if I could, I do not believe this would be a good choice.

So then, for you, what is a good choice?

I journey with two groups of children in view of the sacraments. I do not want children to ask the catechist on the day of their First Communion, 'Who is that one?' as it happened in the case of one of my colleagues... But my priority is to be first with the laypersons committed to catechesis.

How do you live this companionship with the catechists?

First of all, I love them. For me, they are not only members of a 'work force'. We share the same ministry and, in the group of catechists, we live the experience of a Church community. As priest, I am a sign of unity.

And this relationship allows you to journey with them in a concrete way?

Absolutely. Together we live a kind of ongoing formation at the grass roots level, if I dare say, starting from what is lived in the catechetical groups. My role is to authenticate what is being done, but also to challenge, to foster a deeper understanding. I have noticed that catechists who are not accompanied in their work are soon out of breath. They lack spiritual and human nourishment and resources.

In short, this time devoted to the catechists is not wasted?

Far from it! It is really 'consecrated' time, and like everything that is consecrated, it bears fruit and gives life.

And for the children on the whole, are you not... a stranger?

I don't think so. First, precisely, because I know the catechists very well and what they experience with the children. Then this bond allows me to be very present and to take my place as priest in the celebrations and the major days of the Liturgical year lived with the children.

Appropriation

As a team, priests and laypersons, express your reactions. What is your situation? Your options? How are you preparing for the future?

16. Being a child...

Jesus:
'Let the little children come to me.
For it is to such as these
that the Kingdom of God belongs.'
Mk 10:14-16

'Each child is unique.'

'He already has his own character.'

'The child is not a reduced model of an adult.'

'They especially need love and role models.'

'The child has a personal response to give to the unique call of God.'
Synod of Bishops 1977

'They have ideas! They can realize many things.'

'Your children are not your children. (...) They come through you
but not from you.'
K. Gibran

Appropriation

1. Reflect on each statement on this page... What do you think of them? Do you see any practical consequences?
2. Can you 'complete the chart' by adding other affirmations which seem important to you? Can you illustrate them with some examples?
3. Think of your own childhood... Does your experience correspond to some of these statements? If so, you could make note of these and share them.
4. Now look at the questions on the next page. Keeping in mind certain children you know, can you answer some of these questions?
5. From your answers to the previous question, do you see different 'categories' of children taking form? Which ones?

... today, at home

Do they live
with their parents?

Do they have
brothers and sisters?

How do they live:
lodging? food?
communication?
leisure activities?

Immigrants?

What games do they
play? What do they
dream of?

What can their image
of the world possibly be?
of life? of the family?
of God? of themselves?

And television,
how many hours a week?
What do they watch?
Do they talk about that?

Do they have any
pocket money?
How much?

Other persons
in close relation with the child?
What do they experience
in this relationship?

Appropriation (continued)

6. In your opinion, are there other good questions to ask ourselves about what characterizes the children of today in our midst?
7. Think of the children you care for. Trace their 'portrait' with the help of the questions on this page.
8. Now let your eye and mind wander back and forth between these two pages. Do you see any links emerging between a certain statement of the previous page and a particular question on this page? Which ones?
9. In what way do certain statements (previous page) shed light or challenge certain questions (this page)? and vice versa?
10. Using all this material, fill out an 'identity card' for each child in your group, a card you will complete as you have encounters with him or her (cf ch. 26, No 1).

17. At the crossroads of influences

They were going to name him Zechariah after his father. But his mother said, 'No; he is to be called John' [that is: gift of God]... And all of them were amazed. 'What then will this child become?' Lk 1:59-66

We are all products! Products of heredity, of an education, of all sorts of influences and experiences... As the saying goes, each one carries his own bundle from the moment of his birth.

In this bundle, there are treasures but surely burdens as well... or dynamite, even radioactive wastes!

But we are living and conscious products, always in the process of change. In other words, we have a part in the production of ourselves. We are perhaps our main architects. Perhaps?... For it could be that an Other is taking care of us and is yet more interested in us than we are in ourselves!

Could God be the secret of our evolution? Could he succeed in accomplishing this feat of strength that consists in giving us a direction without manipulating us? By the sole virtue of an incomparable love? Might he be the great magnetic force capable of drawing us to him while having an infinite respect for us?

At the crossroads of influences, might there be, not apoliceman with his notebook of misdeeds, but the Friend who is waiting for us to journey along with us?

God is love. Created in his image, each one of us can exercise a loving influence. The education we give can be a loving influence through the grace of God.

Fascinated as we are by the spectacular influences which seem to be manipulating any and everybody: mass media, social pressures, let us take care not to forget or minimize this beneficial influence we can have on each other, particularly in the educative activity. And yet, if we reflect on our own lives, on what has really left a mark on us, is it not the presence or the personal action of this or that man, of this or that woman?

Appropriation

1. Do the exercise on the next page. What do you find? What do you think of that?
2. As for yourself, who had a positive influence on you? How?... Probe the memory of your heart: there are names, faces which made you 'exist'... You can draw your own 'card of life-giving relationships': write your name, the names of persons who have helped you or who are helping you live... what was revealed to you in these relationships... There are also persons for whom you are a 'life-giving relationship'... note them as well.
3. There are 'influences that stifle freedom' and others that make it grow. Make note of examples of each... Look for a passage in the Gospels which sheds a particular light on this subject.

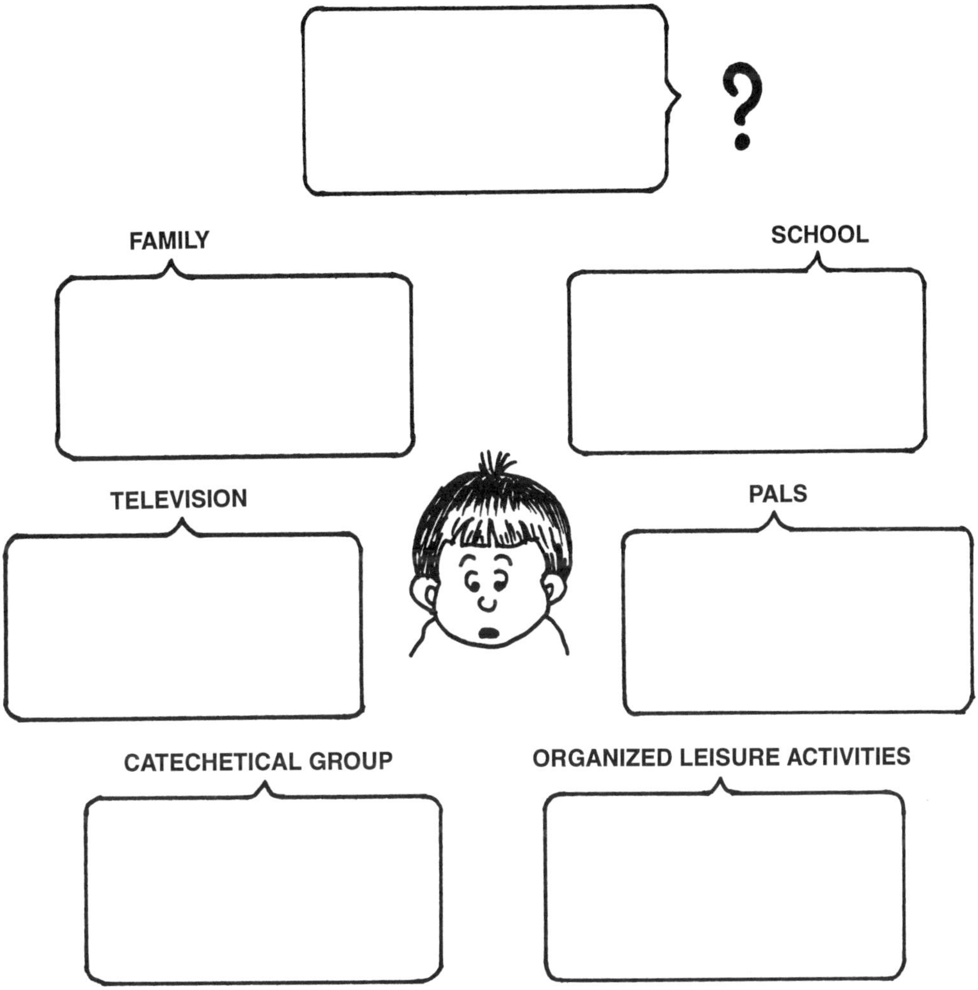

Living is to...

Every 'milieu of life' transmits many diverse experiences and values to the child. By calling upon your concrete knowledge of children, note the most characteristic experiences and values of each milieu mentioned above, such as you perceive them. Check these with friends, colleagues, children.

What are the riches and limitations of each of those realities? How can you enrich what is limited? Make wholesome what is unwholesome?

What could a catechetical group give that is worthy of being lived? How? What good experiences have you already had?

18. Places in which to live and be Church

Everything they owned was held in common.
Acts 4:32

To be born in faith is to be born in the community, in the Church. To live faith is to live the Church. That is true for everyone, children, young people, adults. This is not about a theoretical truth, but about a most concrete experience to be lived.

Normally, the Christian family is the place for the first and fundamental Church experience. But how many children live this reality? And even those to whom this opportunity is given will very soon be confronted, outside the family circle, with other ways of living and thinking.

The large parish community offers everyone a network giving them the sense of belonging, a network of communion and celebration. Adults and children meet in the Sunday gatherings. The great stages of Christian life are lived there.

But the child, still more than the adult, needs relay communities to live and strengthen his faith with children of his own age: prayer, action and mutual help groups; Christian movements; other groups having an authentic educative concern integrating the spiritual dimension.

In this work, we especially wish to draw your attention to the catechesis group and the responsibility of the community which cannot claim it is proclaiming Jesus Christ to the children without offering them concrete locations to 'be Church'.

The children, besides, spontaneously seek life as a group. They need this to discover and affirm their own identity. It is up to us, catechists, to reveal to them progressively the evangelical and ecclesial dimension of all life experienced together. It is up to us to lead them to a generous and true experience of togetherness.

Appropriation

1. Examine the next page closely in order to identify clearly the four components of an authentic Christian community.
2. What is or are the Christian community(ies) where you yourself live these four components? Is there one of these components which appears to you to be underdeveloped in your Christian life?
3. And are those four components present in the group of children you direct? Go over the last three months: what signs do you see at the level of relationships (1), of faith sharing (2), of the bond with the 'whole Church' (3), of openness to the world and of testimony (4)? How can you bring about the growth of what is underdeveloped?
4. With other adults, parents and catechists for example, ask yourself if you would not be justified in challenging some of those responsible for your parish (priest, Community Council), in order to respond better to the need the children have for some 'Church spaces'.

A CHRISTIAN COMMUNITY IS

'A person who has given adherence to Jesus Christ by faith... needs to live in communion with those who have taken the same step... That is why the ecclesial community at all levels has a twofold responsibility with regard to catechesis: it has the responsibility of providing for the training of its members, but it also has the responsibility of welcoming them into an environment where they can live as fully as possible what they have learned. Catechesis is likewise open to missionary dynamism...'

John Paul II, CT 24

19. The children's religious experience

Out of the mouths of infants and nursing babies, you have prepared praise for yourself. Mt 21:16

Religious experience: this expression must not be assigned only to such activities as saying one's prayers, going to Church or to catechism. This concerns our whole life. In fact, for a Christian, the whole human experience is a religious experience in the sense that it binds us to God. Whether or not we are aware of this, whether or not we respond to this relationship, God, on his part, does not cease to set a rendezvous with us at the heart of our existence and of our humanity.

The whole life of the child is, fundamentally, imbued with God and destined to flourish in the love of God. From the first to the last moment of existence, God precedes us in the heart of our being and in the heart of those to whom he sends us to reveal him!

The following page invites you to direct your attention to four aspects of the 'religious experience':

1. The most fundamental and vital human experiences, so beneficial that God must surely dwell in them, even if we are not necessarily aware of it...
2. The initiatives, the 'strokes of genius' of the Holy Spirit manifesting themselves in the words and actions of the child...
3. The profound, sometimes astonishing, questions that the child asks himself about life, death, God... and how he asks them...
4. Everything the child receives as images or ideas of God... a mosaic where the best can intermingle with the worst...

But before going on to the next page, we invite you to do the exercise below. It will help you to see things from within your own experience.

Appropriation

Discover again the principal stages of your human and spiritual evolution, particularly when you were a child (3/4, 7/8, 9/10, 11/12 years old...) Try to go over your existence as a child keeping in mind the four aspects described above: rediscover your vital experiences, your spiritual intuitions, your profound questions, your images and ideas of God... Rediscover all this as concretely as possible: see again the places where you were, the people around you... recall the words, the faces, your emotions... How do you grasp all that today?... What still dwells in you? What, in your opinion, is constructive?... Can you talk about this with anyone?

1. What are the vital experiences indwelt by God even without our being aware of them being so?

2. Do you know of any 'strokes of genius' of the Holy Spirit in the life of a child (intuition, words, prayer, behaviour...)? If so, make note of a few examples.

3. Have you heard children asking astounding questions, so remote and profound? For example...

4. The child has 'absorbed God' in all the situations in which he has been involved! Make a list of the expressions you have heard which seem to be vehicles for more or less questionable images or ideas on God.

As you think of the children you know, note a few elements of response in the above frames. In order to be concrete, focus your attention on a precise age group. You can do the exercise for different ages by reproducing this page. It is worthwhile to compare your answer with others, to check it with competent and experienced people.

Compare what you find in the four frames. What do you think of this? Can you draw some practical guidelines from this?

20. A being in the process of growth

The child grew and became strong... and the favour of God was upon him. Lk 2:40

What can be more spectacular and more amazing than the growth of a child! The parents, astonished, sometimes baffled, never come to the end of discovering their child's progress. Progress in all areas: physical strength and mobility, the capacity of feeling and communicating, intelligence and understanding, know-how and knowing-how-to-be.

The child develops from his own inwardness. A power of life is at work, it does not come from us, educators or parents. But still, our role is important: difficult and demanding, great and beautiful. We are the indispensable partners of the child who is building himself up by responding to the calls of Life of which we can be the actors and the instruments.

Whether this be in the family, whether this be in catechesis or elsewhere, authentic education is always global and complete: it is a service to the person in all the dimensions of his or her existence. The chart on the opposite page hopes to evoke that. As we outline a few stages of the development and of the religious education, we especially want to invite the educators to bring all the aspects into play, to bring out the importance of all the resources.

Appropriation

1. Make the first column of the chart (next page) practical by recalling memories of your own childhood and your experience as parent or educator. (The stages indicated in the chart are neither absolute nor universal. They can, nevertheless, serve as guidelines.)
2. Do the same exercise for the second column. Do not hesitate to give shades of meaning, to complete, to alter according to what you have experienced with the children.
3. The third column deserves special attention. First, try to have a good grasp of the movement from the bottom up, then of the link joining each stage with the others.
4. Think of your own religious education and compare it with the indications in the third column.
5. By taking the third column as a guide for reflection, can you identify some possible mishaps of religious education:
   (a) through the failure of building a 'superior' phase on the roots of the 'inferior' ones;
   (b) through lack of stimulation and help to move from an 'inferior' to a 'superior' phase;
   (c) through failing to 'go back' from a 'superior' phase to a renewed 'inferior' one.

	THE CHILD	...GOD? FAITH?	EDUCATION
Age 11-12	He has a new capacity and a new need to understand and think. He can make choices and commit himself. He lives through many experiences with his pals.	What is believed may be explored by the intelligence. Believing is also choosing and assuming responsibilities with others.	Informing, stimulating, reflecting, fostering understanding... Inviting to make choices and commitments... sustaining fidelity...
Age 9-10	He is curious about everything. He needs to make, to see and to touch. He plays to have fun, to learn, to communicate, 'to try' to play roles and characters.	God is knocking at my door: faith may be lived in a more personal way. The child can pray 'on his own'... ... but he has a strong need of 'being with'.	Fostering and respecting a personal faith. Sustaining the discovery of a vocation. Forming a link and a communion.
Age 6-8	His world of relationships expands... from the family to the 'gang'and companions. His imagination is always in command, but he experiences the shock of reality which is putting up some resistance! So many questions!	Creative? Eternal? A taste for mystery...	Evoking God in his mystery. Telling the stories of Jesus and the Bible. Inviting to communicate with God through prayer, gestures and words.
Age 4-5	The child discovers itself as boy or girl... It experiences the emotions of love and 'hate'... It affirms itself by imitating... and by putting up some opposition.	Is God a Super-Parent? Powerful? Protective? Dangerous?	Offering a fair relationship ('I am with you but I am not you') which allows to exist.
Age 0-3	It lives by being fed, touched, protected. It lives off looks, smells, sounds of voices which are a presence to it.	God is perceived in a confused way (but really given!), made present by those who are present to the child.	Accepting and protecting life. Being present... and for that, being simply and purely... 'in truth'!

The educative attitudes (right column) cannot be substituted one for the other. Each 'superior level' implies being rooted in all the 'inferior ones'. At the top, the flourishing of flowers and fruit, at the bottom, the roots and a fertile soil. Education projects the whole tree. Whoever hopes for fruit works on the roots.

21. Learning

How can I [learn], unless someone guides me?
Acts 8:31

Religious pedagogy draws from the fabulous riches of a tradition of more than a millennium. It also benefits from the recent discoveries of the sciences of education. It would be pretentious and pointless to summarize all that in a few pages. On the other hand, these reminders concerning the pedagogical 'rules of the art' will be useful.

1. We learn only that which corresponds to a vital need

You may lead a horse to water but you cannot make him drink, says the proverb. Identifying the vital needs and responding to them at the right moment and in a proper manner: such is the beginning (and the end) of all pedagogy. Needs vary with age and persons. Nevertheless, by drawing upon certain works of research (Maslow), we will readily point out the following needs:

- physiological needs (food, care, sleep, physical activity...)
- need for security (psychological, emotional...)
- need for integration (being part of a group...)
- need to be acknowledged (to be recognized for what we really are...)
- need to understand and give meaning to what we live
- need to 'fulfil oneself' and grow
- need to communicate and share.

Theoretically, the elementary needs (top of the list) must be met in order that the others may be as well. But this is not an absolute rule. At a given moment, to communicate may be more important than to eat...

2. Learning concerns the whole being

Distinctions are often made concerning the following areas:

- KNOWING (information, knowledge, understanding...)
- KNOWING-HOW (skills and aptitudes to do and act...)
- KNOWING-HOW-TO-BE (personal fulfilment and capacity to communicate...).

The important point in pedagogy is to integrate these three dimensions, whatever may be the apparent domain in which the educative action is taking place. For instance, the appropriation of information (knowing) never goes without some affective repercussions (knowing-how-to-be) of this information nor without the manner of transmitting it.

3. **We learn better by doing than by listening**

Without giving an absolute value to the following statistics (they are in order of magnitude), experience shows that we retain:

- 10-20% of what we have read or heard
- 30-40% of what we have seen and heard
- 50% of what we have seen/read/heard and discussed with others
- 60-70% of what we have done
- 80% of what we have sought and discovered on our own
- 90-100% of what we have found with effort, having borne the brunt of the work... or what has elicited from us a deep sense of awareness (decisive experiences, sometimes triggered off by very little: a word or gesture experienced at the right moment).

4. **And yet the word is absolutely necessary**

It is through language that we move from a kind of raw experience to a more conscious one, truly a part of ourselves. A large portion of education consists in providing precise words to the child, so that he may identify, clarify, deepen and assimilate his living experience. When it is said and heard within a relationship of trust, the word leads from the experience to a renewed experience:

EXPERIENCE → WORD WITHIN A RELATIONSHIP → GROWING AWARENESS

Hence the importance of 're-reading' what has been experienced.

5. **The learning process grows especially through positive reinforcement**

The affirmations are the sanctions of the learning process. Negative affirmations like punishments, low marks. Positive affirmations: rewards or good marks. We would especially like to insist on the effectiveness of positive affirmations which are not artificially made up by the adult ('be nice and you will have a chocolate'), but which are the natural consequence of the child's behaviour:

- pleasure derived from the activity itself (well-being: physical and psychological...)
- pride in having achieved something, in being aware of a result
- acknowledgement from others (adults, companions, community...)

The summit of education is probably to do everything to set up a pedagogy based on success and positive affirmation. Even in failures, apparent or real: through these painful experiences, paths of hope and progress can open up for the child inasmuch as he reads such promises in the eye of the educator (cf chapter 36).

6. **Learning processes experienced in depth are personalized, secret and radiant**

By this heading, somewhat enigmatic, we wish to say that the knowing-how-to-be (learning process in depth) is not learned by conditioning or training (these elements, at the very most, can contribute to it), but:

– by an intimate evolution, proper to each person. True pedagogy will thus consist more in winning over the other, in drawing close to his secret, in adapting myself to him rather than adapting him to myself;

– the essential is not necessarily the most spectacular. All that takes place in the innermost secret of the heart and of an evolution, like germination. The visible effects may appear only long after the sowing;

– every time the person's 'heart is touched', a radiant source of life lights up forever in that person. If I have experienced a true forgiveness once in my life, I will never forget it and my whole being will be transformed by it. In pedagogy, it is better 'to strike home' than to accumulate superficial interventions (cf p. 74, No. 7).

Appropriation

1. For each of the six 'rules of the art' listed, look for at least one example in your own experience of being educated.
2. For each of these examples, analyze the process by answering the following questions:
   (a) Did the stakes of the learning process correspond to a vital need? Which one?
   (b) From what point did you start this learning process (did you start from zero or from further on?)
   (c) What step, what progress did you make at that time?
   (d) What role did the educator (a 'qualified' educator or just a companion) play?
   (e) Did this learning process leave any traces in you? What are they?
3. Share this with other people.
4. Go over these same exercises but, this time, by reviewing experiences you have had as an educator.
5. Throughout all this research and through your experience, do you detect other 'rules of the art'? If so, state them and check them with other educators.
6. Along with other catechists and with the priest accompanying your group, ask yourselves to what extent all these 'rules of the art' suit religious education. Restate them as need be and bring out those about which you agree and which could constitute in some way your common charter for educators, your scale of evaluation.
7. Read the following text and make up an exercise which would allow you to discuss it and draw something from it for your own practical use.

Forward with the music!

How can you make someone develop a liking for music? A question of capital importance for any catechist...

...There was once a learned music professor. He knew everything about music and spoke admirably about classical and modern works.

One day, a student, a dunce, asked him:

– Sir! I brought a record... could we listen to it?

– No time, said the professor.

Another student was punished because he was whistling the Hymn to Joy under his breath while the professor was explaining Beethoven.

After years of teaching, this professor had doubts. He made a long journey throughout the world to observe other professors and discover how music was taught elsewhere. He also visited the great conservatories as well as folklore groups or musicians of certain primitive tribes.

When he returned home, he had to take to his bed, so tired was he from his trip. A few weeks later he died. On his bedside table, a small notebook was found in which he had written the essential points of his discoveries. Here is what he had written:

'In order to develop a liking for music in anyone, one must love it himself. There is a melody singing in everyone's heart. The good professor is the one who knows the music of his own heart. The good professor rejoices when he hears someone else singing a tune coming from his heart, even if he himself would sing things in another way.

'The most important point is not to speak about music but to make music heard. The professor will not hesitate to hum his favourite songs or softly whistle a simple melody running through his head. But a professor is not necessarily a good singer nor a brilliant instrumental performer. In addition to his own songs, he will not forget to make his students listen to some great performances... Ah! the records and the cassettes...

'And especially, most especially, the professor should be all ears to hear the simple tunes circulating among the students. He should not prevent them from either singing or whistling but, on the contrary, he should encourage and help them make a common melody out of their little tunes.

'He should not fear mistakes or blunders. Better a squawk from students who sing than the deceitful harmony of a class where not the least note is ever heard.

'The professor will think he has taught with success when he learns that his students sing softly in the street and whistle in their bathtubs.'

As they read these lines, the heirs had various reactions:

– The poor man, he had lost his mind!

– The good it did to spend so much money and travel so far to say such things!

– He is botching all our teaching!

– And suppose he were right?...

Some said nothing but went away humming... something they had not done since they had obtained their diplomas!...

Michel Salamolard.
Vie, January 1984

22. On the way to an integral education

Not everyone who says to me, 'Lord, Lord', will enter the kingdom of heaven, but only the one who does the will of my Father. Mt 7:21

In this chapter, we will deal especially with education inasmuch as it elicits and sustains the existential becoming of the person, the moral and spiritual (knowing-how-to-be) development of that person.

The person is one, and all the types of learning processes are, therefore, interconnected. As you are making distinctions between the various types of learning processes, we ask you not to separate them, but to differentiate them the better to bring out their complementary interplay.

The common aspects of all the learning processes

Whatever be the level (knowing, knowing-how, knowing-how-to-be) considered, the learning process can always be described as one in which someone acquires a new capacity. The stages of this process are the following:

The 'return' arrow indicates that the process never comes to an end. A successful learning process leads one to be motivated to go further (reinforcement).

First type of learning process: **knowing**

The school will be discussed later. Here, let us be satisfied with schematizing:

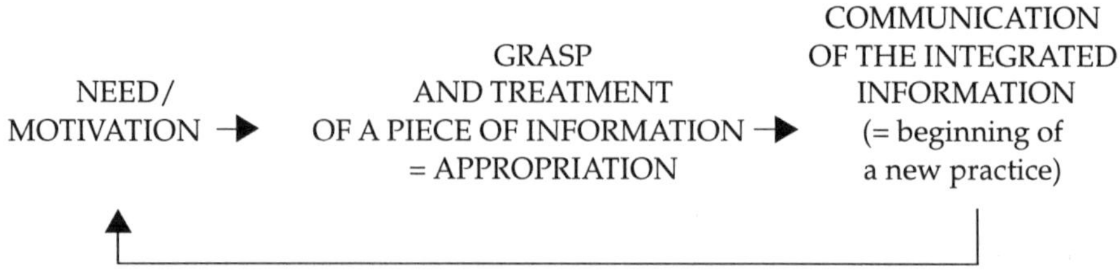

As in all learning processes, the educator plays a role in the three stages.

Second type of learning process: **knowing-how**

This is about learning gestures and behaviours, for example, painting, making a sign of the cross, arranging flowers, miming the Our Father, swimming...

NEED/ MOTIVATION →	IMITATION REPEATED EXERCISES → (+ explanations)	SUCCESSFUL PRACTICE (and gratifying)

(with a return arrow from SUCCESSFUL PRACTICE back to NEED/MOTIVATION)

We can see the central role of the model, for example the educator and his way of doing things, and of the exercises, or studies of situations: working through trials, errors, and tentative efforts is more effective than simple injunctions ('make your sign of the cross!') or explanations (even if these have their importance).

When well directed, a visit to a church will better introduce to prayer than a theory, no matter how excellent.

'I teach my catechists,' someone was saying, 'never to have to say "Be quiet" to the children when they visit a church, but to do what is necessary for the children to feel good in silence.'

Third type of learning process: **knowing-how-to-be**

We suspect that these 'learning processes of the third type' are the most important and the most demanding. Less so than for the others, can we give recipes here.

By drawing our inspiration from certain researchers who have studied the phenomena of influence (Kelman, Parsons, Chazel) we shall attempt to open up a few avenues.

As a whole, the learning process of the third type can be visualized as follows:

NEED/ MOTIVATION →	IDENTIFICATION with a PERSON EMBODYING certain VALUES + INTERIORIZATION of these values (awareness + exercises) →	PERSONAL GROWTH AND DEVELOPMENT

(with a return arrow from PERSONAL GROWTH AND DEVELOPMENT back to NEED/MOTIVATION)

A few comments will help you enter into the understanding of this process which is simple only on paper!

1. In this learning process, it is a matter of integrating values, of developing spiritual attitudes (for example: joy, gratitude, service, etc.). The first requirement consists of being clear about what has value for the human being, what can constitute a life project for him. We take the liberty of referring you back to chapter 7... and to the gospel.

2. This learning process deals not only with exterior behaviour patterns but with the heart of being. We might as well say that such an evolution is mysterious and intimate. We do not know its secret 'laws' and we have no hold on them (fortunately!). Everything ultimately takes place in the mystery where a free human being is reached by the Spirit of God.

3. The identification with a person embodying values is something other than a simple mime. I see someone living an ideal which is attractive to me and awakens in me the desire to live in my own way in the same spirit. I feel I will be happy if I act 'like that person, in a way different from that person's way'. That is what is meant when we talk about imitating Jesus or a particular saint. It is also the meaning of the: 'Go and do likewise' of Luke 10:37. Identification supposes a contact with the person to whom I refer myself, but this contact can take extremely diverse forms: physical contact, surely, but also mental, psychological, spiritual, and symbolic contact.

4. Interiorization consists in making the values I have perceived in someone else my own. It is not a matter of having some sort of foreign body enter into myself, but of allowing something already there to awaken and grow in me, like a seed, and that contact with the other has revealed to me and continues to reveal to me: I see realized in that person something that is in me in the state of a promise or a seed. The gaze on the other (identification) leads me into my self (interiorization). Prayer plays a role of capital importance here, as well as the experience of silence and meditation.

5. When two or more peoplemeet and share their experience of values, they become a community where the experience of each is stimulated and sustained by the others. A living Church!

6. In the wake of some researchers (Moscovici, Abric), we would like to stress the influence of the representation system on attitudes and behaviours. The image I have of myself, of others, of life, of the world, of God (= system of representations) determines in part my way of life and action. Here we find again the necessary connection between the cognitive learning processes (knowing) and the existential learning processes (knowing-how-to-be). We have already said as much: the WORD (not just any word), within a RELATIONSHIP (not just any one) is effective: it leads to the awareness and to the renewal of the experience (chapter 21).

7. Knowledge, or the representation, is an active process of the subject which, in this way, builds 'his world'. The intuitions of the so-called neo-cognitivistic currents seem particularly interesting to us in this sense, with the concepts of auto-organization, of the emergence of global states, of 'enaction', of contextuality (cf for example, F. J. Varela, Connaître. These views should be compared with those, set on another level, of P. Berger and Th. Luckmann (cf p. 107).

Scholars (Piaget, Kohlberg) attempted to understand and describe the moral development of the child. From these studies, we suggest that you remember three great stages which appear enlightening to us.

First stage: The action is strongly linked with submission to the parents or to other persons having the power to reward or punish, be it only by 'turning away', by ceasing to love.

Second stage: The action is strongly bound by the conformity to expectations and norms of a reference group (family, peers, race...)

Third stage: The action proceeds from within the person, from the values the person has freely chosen to embody.[1]

We are now in a better position to grasp the role of the educator in the moral development of the child. In this sense, an educator is the man or woman who:

1. Offers him or herself as a person embodying values. For a Christian, that supposes a life 'turned to Christ' (cf 1 Cor 11:1), the incarnation of all values. Identifying myself with him (Eucharist!) allows me to become myself, makes me truly free.
2. Offers the child the attention and the relationship allowing him to 'take the step', to take the risk with confidence in the direction of a call. Moral development is a continuous process of death and rebirth. In order that the child might die to a situation of death (for example, egotism, revenge), he needs to hear that life is what is calling him further on. This call is in the voice, the gaze, the person of the educator knowing not only how to order but also how to make what he orders possible.
3. Puts in touch with the Christ of the Gospels and with the saints (canonized or not) who are like him.

Appropriation

1. Recall a person who has embodied values for you and at whose contact you have experienced the desire to 'become better'. What contacts did you have with this person? What was this person doing? What did you feel?
2. Go back to the three attitudes referred to above as being characteristics of the educator's role and ask yourself: when and how did I find this attitude in anyone? When and how did I play this role for others?
3. In your recent practice, do you have an example of the learning process of the first and the second types (knowing and knowing-how)? Do you rediscover these stages outlined above?
4. In catechesis, how can the three types of learning processes be connected?

1. For a more complete presentation of Kohlberg's theory, cf CNER, Formation chrétienne des adultes, pp. 120-122, DDB 1986.

Pointers for an education of the conscience

1. The essential point is the personal contact with Christ encountered in the Gospel and in prayer.

2. There is also the personal contact with people who are like Jesus.

3. It is of prime importance to know the child well, his system of values, the experiences through which he has structured this system.

4. The catechetical group is a privileged space in which to live certain values.

5. The educator can help the children to develop a keener sense of moral discernment: by clarifying the motivations and the consequences (for oneself, for others) of this or that mode of action. Stories, case studies, role-playing, can be useful in this perspective.

6. The personal dialogue with a child is a privileged means of educating the conscience... and trust.

7. Jesus' attitude is characterized by an immense hope which calls sinners, and a vast mercy that never demeans, that respects the humble journeys and ultimately allows one to exist! To educate is to offer this same attention to the child.

8. There is a specific sacrament which celebrates the forgiveness of Christ offering a new lease on life. It behaves the priest, by virtue of his ministry, to be a privileged witness of mercy.

Underlying these orientations is a lever ordering all moral education: it is the quality of relationships offered to the child. To communicate in truth, to love, is more effective than moralizing.

Appropriation

1. For each of the above 'pointers', look for ways of living it in education. Share these with your team.
2. All of the present chapter is important: it is worth 'studying in depth'. Make note of what you remember and what raises questions for you. Share these with your team and with the priest accompanying you. Share the essential points of your convictions and experiences with the group. Decide how you will pursue the reflection.

Watch for possible slips in moral education!

1. **The temptation is to impose a morality through constraint and fear**. By this means, we obtain submission and the appearance of values. Appearance alone. Everything will collapse when constraint ceases, unless the latter is interiorized, and we will then see the tragedy of falsified or morbid consciences. That becomes serious when God is invoked to reinforce the constraint and the fear. 'If you are naughty, God, who sees everything, will punish you...'

2. **Similarly, it is tempting to attribute our imperfect feelings to God**. 'When you lie, you hurt Jesus...' We thus reinforce the confusion the child easily makes between God and grown-ups. For the child, hurting his parents means the threat of being deprived of their love. He hears his father or mother telling him sometimes in anger: 'you are unbearable... how you can get on my nerves!' By playing with the child's feelings ('hurting Jesus... making him angry'), we risk stunting his growth.

3. **So what should be said about God in the domain of moral education**? Very simply, the truth: 'God loves you, he wants you to be happy and to grow in his love. When you do wrong, and that happens to you as it does to me, God gives you still a greater love so that you may again begin to be happy.'

4. **The whole vocabulary of sin can become a formidable pitfall**. The small child is not yet in a position to distinguish the difference between what is a sin, a mistake or simply an imperfection. Everything is incomplete in him. In comparison with what is presented to him as 'ideal', he is 'small', and that is entirely normal. Neither can he see the difference between the phantasms of his ideas and his wilful intentions. What a chaos in his head! Therefore, we shall not insist on sin. It is better to note, with the child, that he sometimes does wrong, and to give him progressively some point of reference so he can find himself again between good and evil, between what is voluntary and what is not, between what is free and what is not. We are not saying that we must not talk about sin, but a good discernment is the proper thing so that the child may progressively make the distinction between the voluntary failings of his simple imperfections and, especially, so that he may discover that his way of living cannot be separated from his relationship with God.

5. **All this is particularly important in relation to the sacrament of forgiveness**. We think that the child has the right to receive at a very early age the sign of God's mercy and tender love through the sacramental ministry of the Church. But, again, what a betrayal if that became a countersign leading to a morbid sense of guilt and a distorted image of God. Assuredly, it would be preferable not to attempt anything. The emphasis, therefore, will be placed on God calling with love and raising with tenderness. The more the child will be in touch with that God, the more his conscience will awaken by itself in the movement of the Holy Spirit.

23. Leading as Jesus does

Be imitators of me, as I am of Christ. 1 Cor 11:1

In this chapter, we want to trace the broad lines of a pedagogy according to the gospel. We propose that you contemplate Christ as an educator by following Luke's Gospel.

1. **In order to be an educator, Jesus lets himself be educated by God**

Jesus is, par excellence, the one led by an Other, the one who constantly receives himself from an Other he calls Father – precisely because the latter makes him live – and from whom he receives and communicates the Spirit. This experience of Jesus is suggested in different ways:

- Jesus receives his education from God through the humble educative activity of Mary and Joseph (2:51) as well as through the whole tradition of his human and religious community (2:46);
- his experience is unique and personal, but it is part of a precise initiative of his time (3:21-22);
- he lets the Spirit lead him up to the most decisive choices (4:1-13);
- in the secret of a personal prayer, he lets himself be educated from within his relationship with God (3:21; 5:16; 6:12; 9:18, 28-29; 10:21; 11:1; 22:32, 40, 46; 23:34, 46);
- he lives his life as a mission which is part of the salvation project God had revealed in Scripture (4:17-21);
- to the limit, unto the night of faith, he chooses to be faithful to the Father (22:42) to whom he totally surrenders himself (23:46).

2. **He expresses God through his whole being and his whole life: deeds and words**

We can see this agreement between the being and the expression of Jesus throughout the whole Gospel. It is particularly evident in chapter 15: Jesus' words reveal the meaning and the impact of what he does. Moreover, his language itself (parables) respects the mystery of God and the freedom of his listeners, all the while inviting them to a new vision, a new and deeper experience.

3. **He meets and educates each one in a personal way**

To be sure, Jesus addresses the crowds. But it is within very personal encounters that his educative action is more pronounced. Luke strongly emphasizes these encounters. Jesus does not apply any ready-made recipes to them. He greets each one in his truth and in the situation he is in. He answers his questions and provokes him (without doing him violence) to make the step which is possible for him today. Read in this perspective: 7:36-50; 10:25-37; 19:1-10; 22:61; 23:39-43.

4. **He establishes a particular relationship with the Twelve**

Jesus calls them personally (5:1-11; 6:12-16), but he does not necessarily choose a pious and learned elite (5:27-32).

With them, he will live an experience of living together, progressively communicating who he is to them, in daily life but also in privileged moments (9:18-22; 9:28-36). He educates them by entrusting responsibilities to them (9:1-6) and by making them reflect on what they have experienced (evaluation!) (9:49-50). He makes them discover gradually a clearly oriented style of life and way of being and educating (9:46-48; 22:24-27).

5. **He is not afraid to demand much while respecting their freedom**

Those who approach Jesus enter into a climate in which the highest demands go hand in hand with the greatest freedom. Jesus calls in a decisive way without ever manipulating. His requirements are those of love (9:57-62; 18:18-30).

6. **He educates to prayer starting from his own experience of prayer**

The disciples see Jesus pray, now recollected in a silence of plenitude, now letting his praise spring forth. They wish to share this prayer so simple and so true: 'Lord, teach us to pray.' (10:21-24; 11:1-13).

7. **He casts on each a gaze which makes one exist and grow**

You have probably noticed this throughout the reading of all the texts describing encounters. Re-read particularly in this perspective: 7:48; 15:1-2; 19:7-9; 23:43. Jesus' gaze opens heaven to sinners.

8. **Even down to the apparent failure of his mission, he remains faithful to the passion of his life: to give the love of God so that man may live**

Jesus was not at all understood by his disciples, at least before Easter. At the moment of his death, his educative action seems to be a total failure, as much with the crowds as with his friends who abandon him and turn back disillusioned (24:17) to their old habits. Easter is what changed everything. Did not Jesus have to go (24:26) to the limit of the gift of himself, in the failure of the Passion, so that the eyes of his disciples might be opened and their hearts be kindled... until then, all they had received from Jesus was, so to speak, frozen?

Appropriation

1. For the indicated passages and for others (a beautiful opportunity to make a continuous reading of all of Luke's gospel!), use the scale of evaluation suggested in the last chapter (cf p. 75, exercise 2).
2. Have you ever met people who were for you 'educators like Jesus'? Recall what you experienced with them...
3. You may prolong your study and discover the educative and educated Church by making the same kind of reading in the Acts of the Apostles (by the same author, Luke). Begin, for example, by studying 8:26-40 or 10:1-11, 18.
4. Go back over the two previous chapters and ask yourself: to what extent does Jesus' way lead us further on or otherwise?

24. The objectives of catechesis for children

So that my joy may be in you. Jn 15:11

The main sights of a catechesis for children clearly stand out in CT 37. Here is a display of John Paul II's thought:

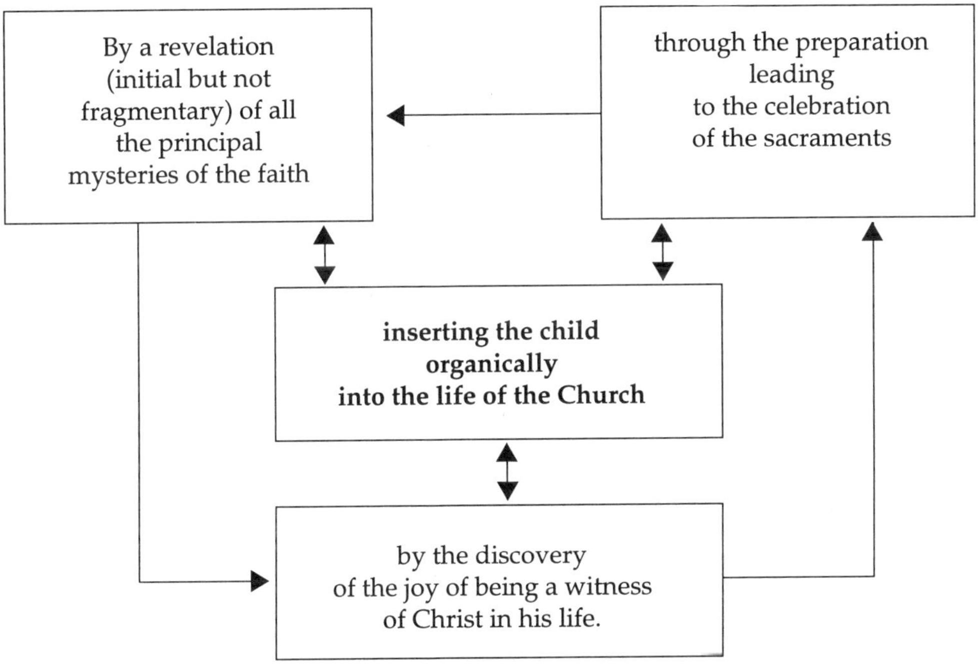

This catechesis, says the pope, has 'a living dimension that keeps it from remaining merely doctrinal' (cf chapter 28).

We will come back to these elements in the next chapter.

Appropriation

Decipher and make the above plan your own with the help of the following questions:

- What is principally at stake? Take a good look at what is at the centre...
- In the three sights flowing from this centre, do you recognize the 'structure of the Christian experience' (cf chapter 10): Word, Memory, Testimony?
- Does the catechesis in your parish give a rightful place to the above objectives? With what emphasis? With what lack of emphasis?

In order not to separate what God has united – the Revelation in and through what is vital in life – we think it useful to give you a general view of the educative sights such as they appear in recent studies.

1. Educate today for tomorrow

To educate is to lead the child to the adult state, by taking into account the fact that, tomorrow, he will be an adult living in a new world, and not yesterday, in a traditional world (P. Osterrieth, *Faire des adultes*, p. 24, Dessart and Mardaga, 1976).

It is sometimes a good thing to restate these obvious elements to ourselves! And to draw consequences from them.

The world of tomorrow will be a pluralist one. To be a Christian will not be taken for granted. The children of today will be confronted with unbelief, atheism, religious visions of 'every colour'. They will have to face ethical and social challenges of which we already have a glimpse. It would be hardly responsible on our part to prepare them for a 'soft Christianity'. But it would be no better to make of them hardened and intransigent sectarians.

To educate for tomorrow in catechesis means:

- **to develop a taste for the essential and the true;**
- **to grow roots rather than to accumulate;**
- **to accept boldly and confidently the necessary confrontations rather than to fear doubts, struggles and difference.**

Counter-solutions or how to form 'future ex-Christians'

In your catecheses, act as if:

- a Christian is never touched by doubts and never questions matters of faith;
- to believe is taken for granted;
- the 'foundation' of faith is to have clear-cut ideas and indisputable principles;
- to have an experience of faith above all is to experience intense feelings of peace, fulfilment, of a warm environment free of all conflict;
- when one 'knows' the whole doctrine, 'applying it' is but a matter of the will...

Appropriation

In the perspective of this paragraph, play with your team the game of 'solutions and counter-solutions' on this theme: how to train Christians today for tomorrow... A sheet of paper, two columns... after some time, explain the image you have made for yourselves of: the world of tomorrow, of what it will mean to be a Christian, of catechesis.

2. At the service of the full growth of the child

The success of catechesis for children to a large extent depends on the way it corresponds, or not, to the process of the human development of the child. This development is known. We know what can stimulate or stifle it.

A psychologist, E. H. Erikson, has identified eight periods of 'crisis' throughout the course of life (1 to 4 in childhood, 5 and 6 during adolescence, 7 around the forties, 8 in old age). Each 'crisis' presents an opportunity for growth and a risk of blockage. We are of the opinion that the phenomena described by Erickson are permanent dimensions of the development. There are so many alternatives challenging us to be lucid about our pedagogies: by our manner of doing things, on what side we lay emphasis:

1. **Fundamental trust** – or fundamental mistrust according to whether or not there is a climate of security and the basic needs are met…

2. **Autonomy** – or shame and doubt about one's own personality according to whether or not a fair relationship is established with the educator (unfair attitudes: excessive domination, too much permissiveness)…

3. **Initiative** – or guilt according to whether a balance has been found between 'pleasure' and 'responsibility'…

4. **Creative know-how** – or inferiority according to whether a balance is established between 'performances to bring to success' and the joy of gratuitous relationships... between 'action' and 'relationships'…

5. **Personalization** (identity) – or confusion of identify (not having a clear idea of who I am) according to the possibility the subject has of affirming himself 'from within' and to discover 'himself' by 'trying out' various roles and characters…

6. **The capacity of entering into an intimate relationship with others** – or isolation…

7. **The tendency and capacity of helping others in their becoming** – or stagnation – this, to be sure, is a choice especially for the adult, but the child also, in his way, grows by making others grow…

8. **Acceptation of self**, of one's life as it is... and of the coming of death – or despair and frustration this is especially to come later... but it is already beginning!

3. Directing and developing the live energies of being

From the works of C. Rogers and B. Grom, we identify three fundamental dynamisms which sum up Erickson's stages, in some way, and may become the 'existential place' of the great Christian forces: faith, hope and love

1. TRUST. Because I feel I am accepted as I am, I can accept myself and others as they are. Because I am not judged, I can be in touch with my intimate experience, which is obscure, perturbing, ambivalent... the path of FAITH.

2. The DESIRE TO LIVE. Because I feel secure, I can take risks and discover the world and its wonders. I find that life is good and I can make projects. I can change, grow, transform myself from the 'centre' of my being which I have gradually discovered and inhabited... the path of HOPE.

3. SYMPATHY (empathy) or the capacity of being sensitive to others. Because I myself have been 'reached' and accepted in my emotions and feelings, I can feel, with someone else, his joy, his grief. I can develop interest 'from within myself' to 'within the other'... the path of CHARITY.

A Christian pedagogue, F. Oser, gives us a key to develop these dynamics through the different forces and attitudes they bear. **To lead the child gradually to discover, by living them, the attitudes and the 'living forces' that the word, then, will enlighten and bring to an awareness**. In short: progressively (a), to let live (b), to explain, clarify and (c) make aware. This 'pedagogy of living forces' can be deployed in three mutually linked areas:

(a) forces centred on the very PERSON: for example, to be amazed, to be in wonder, to show respect, self-control...

(b) forces centred on the BODY and LITURGICAL EXPRESSIONS, for example, to make a 'true' gesture of peace, to kneel while being conscious of the significance of this gesture, to open one's hands in a prayerful way...

(c) forces centred on RELATIONSHIPS, for example, being attentive to someone, expressing sympathy, being disposed to cooperate, being responsible..

Appropriation

As a team: Reproduce the chart on page 81. Place it at the centre of a large piece of paper. After a discussion, note all around it the orientations drawn from pp. 86-87. Establish the maximum number of links between these orientations and the elements of the chart, for example: Erickson's 'initiative' seems to fit in well with 'the joy of being a witness to Christ'. Comment. Show this relationship by means of an arrow.

25. The catechetical itinerary of the child

Jesus himself... went with them. Lk 24:15

The itinerary to reach the great objectives of the catechesis for children varies according to dioceses, regions and the textbooks used. It may be altered with time. That is why, rather than an imposed itinerary, we propose to you a map of the places not to be missed. Some of these places must be visited often, others offer a unique experience. Numerous bonds link them all together.

Appropriation

1. With the help of the map, reconstruct the concrete itinerary you used. Check it against the official documents.
2. Within your parish or your region, are there any itineraries that are differentiated in relation to the particular situations of the children? If so, make note of them. If not, is this something that should be promoted? How?
3. There may also be some 'accidents along the way'. Did you ever happen to be a witness of them? How could this be remedied? How could they be avoided?
4. As a team, make an amusing and instructive exercise: stick a reproduction of your map in the middle of a poster; all around, by sticking pictures taken from magazines, make the environment real, such as it is present to you. Then read your panel aloud.

The itinerary before the itinerary

One moment that is often decisive is the one at which the very young child receives the first elements of catechesis from its parents and the family surroundings. These elements will perhaps be no more than a simple revelation of a good and provident Father in heaven to whom the child learns to turn its heart. The very short prayers that the child learns to lisp will be the start of a loving dialogue.(...) I cannot insist too strongly on this early initiation by Christian parents in which the child's faculties are integrated into a living relationship with God. CT 36

FEELING AT HOME IN A CHURCH . . UNDERSTANDING AND BEHAVING
SENSING THE MYSTERY
GOD OF LOVE
FINDING ONESELF WITH OTHERS IN A COMMUNITY OF FAITH
UNDERSTANDING AND LIVING THE LITURGICAL TIMES
EASTER
KNOWING
WHAT HE
WHAT HE HAS DONE
PRAYING IN SECRET
DEVELOPING ONE'S 'LIVING FORCES' IN FAITH, HOPE AND LOVE
FINDING ONESELF AGAIN IN THE BIBLE

WITNESSING IN DAILY LIFE
NG YES FREELY TO
JESUS CHRIST
PRAYING WITH
OTHER CHRISTIANS
TOWARDS AN
UNDERSTANDING
OF THE FAITH
CELEBRATING
FORGIVENESS
EIVING
TISM
TAKING PART
IN THE
EUCHARIST
LIVING
CONFIRMATION
CHS

26. Animating a group of children

Where two or three are gathered in my name, I am there among them. Mt 18:20

Recall the first time you found yourself in front of 'your' group of children... Emotion, curiosity, enthusiasm, anxiety: there was probably something of all that in your heart. You had imagined what they would be like, had dreamt about them, and here they were in front of you – with you! – very much alive, in flesh and blood. There were several of them, but already a germ of unity was taking form, something common to all which, you hoped, would grow. And you in their midst to serve them...

A great adventure is beginning for yourself as for the children. Animating a group is every bit an art and a skill that you gradually acquire in practice. Before considering a few more practical and technical aspects of this art, we take the liberty of reminding you of its spirit within our catechetical perspective.

You will not be wasting your time – much to the contrary! – by re-reading particularly chapters 3 and 18 which propose to you the spiritual, ecclesial, sacramental dimensions of a Christian group.

As you meditate on the opposite page, as well as on the introductory quotation at the top of this page, at one glance you will grasp the essential: the circle evokes a reality, not rigid, unified, with the possibility of expansion; the animator is not the central point; the group is not an island, but a place of encounter, a temporary place within a large space of life.

From the circle to the star: the diagram below presents the more concrete aspects we will consider in the following pages. A star which can already direct your reflection before guiding your practical action...

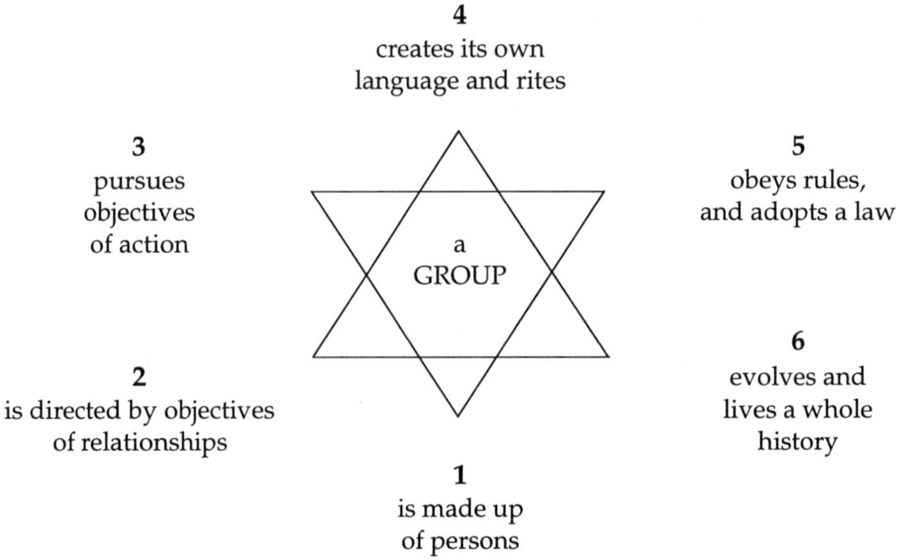

Appropriation

After you have re-read chapters 3 and 18 and meditated on this page, tell each other, as a group (obviously!), what is stirring in you (projects, hope, convictions, experiences, fears?...). Do not get involved in debates. Listen to each other. When all those who wish to have expressed themselves, ask yourselves: are there any points common to all our reactions? Are there any differences (do not try to minimize them)? You may conclude (unless this is a beginning) with a silent prayer or with the Our Father...

1. A group is made up of persons

And children are individuals!

Between the pole of the GROUP and that of PERSONS, the animator often hesitates or experiences a certain tension: to which must preference be given? Some are very attentive to the group, of which they 'sense' the atmosphere and movement, but have all the difficulties in the world remembering who is each child.

Others are concerned about each and everyone, but somewhat neglect the life of the group. Obviously, a good animator tries to play both cards, that of the group and that of the persons. If he tends to place more emphasis on the one or the other, he does so consciously and puts corrective measures in place. By evaluating his own activity with others, he gradually discovers that, far from opposing each other, group and persons mutually make each other exist.

To begin with, let us stress the importance of knowing the children in terms of different persons each in his own place, and of the personal relationship that you can establish and develop with each one of them.

(a) *How to know 'your' children*

We propose that you use a 'personal file' which you build up yourself with your team, like the one on the opposite page. We suggest a few basic elements. Kindly examine them and, as need be, complete and modify them. Also seek the best form of presentation (practical, clear): format, page setting.

Even if, by temperament, you are allergic to the task of making up files, we advise you to practise doing them systematically at least for a period of time (from three to six months): you will increase your capacity to observe and understand.

(b) *Entertain personal relationships with each child*

Here again, we urge you to make up your 'card of relationships' with the help of the suggestions on the opposite page. And we say again to you: try this out; for a few months systematically fill out the file you will have organized.

The re-reading of your files will allow you to have a better knowledge of what you are doing...

> 'The groups I attend to are so numerous that I cannot see how I could still do all this work!' – In that case, try it out with ONE witness group... and again ask yourself the question: who could really give me a hand?
>
> **...and to do better what you know!**

Personal file (do not become an indiscreet investigator)

Mary JAMES, born on... Address and telephone Lives with (family, others) Her school, her class (her integration?) Is a member of the following societies or groups (her integration?) Her friends, boys and girls Her religious life (catechism, sacraments, experiences, reactions, etc.) Her interests, games and favourite pastimes Her health Her projects and dreams Outstanding events in her life Other impressions... questions

↑

(Information may be passed on from one file to another.)

Veronica SMITH			
DATES of our meetings	His messages (words or gestures)	My messages (words or gestures)	To be pursued... in what direction?
Each date is preceded by a letter according to the following code: O Ordinary session of the group C Chance meeting H Meeting through his initiative M Meeting through my initiative			

Relationship card

2. A group is directed by objectives of relationships

Underlying all other objectives, there are relationships: my place in the group? Will I be acknowledged? Liked? Rejected? Who will give orders? Exercise influence? With whom will I get along well? With whom will I have problems? Will there be any atmosphere? Will we have a good time? Will we feel good together?

Everyone (including the animator) has his expectations and fears. All this makes up a vast potential of energy which will circulate, be exchanged... to build or to destroy, to enliven or to cause suffering.

There is the formal structure of the group in which the roles are clearly defined: the animator, the 'animated'... sometimes very lively! There are roles officially assumed by the children (it is important to think of this!): holding the kitty, making the souvenir album, 'recording' the rules and the laws of the group, etc.

There is also the informal structure, of prime importance, that the children organize for themselves. Who is the leader? The star? The scapegoat? The out-and-out clown? Subgroups develop through affinities. There are territorial and power conflicts. There are roles suggested to the animator: leader? referee? father? mother? ally? rival?

To find your place in this and help the children find theirs (the aims are of some stature: communion!) we suggest four tools:

1. The sociogram, empirically constructed (see opposite page) or more technically constructed.
2. The session journal (see opposite page).
3. The re-reading (or evaluation) of the affective and relational experience.

This exercise is simple and effective. It is based on the fact that verbalization of emotions allows the group to live them in a better way. We advise you to do this re-reading systematically at the end of each session (five minutes). From time to time, a longer period will be useful to go further in depth. Two golden rules:

- each is free to speak or not to speak;
- each is listened to (no one interrupts; no one gives advice or expresses his reactions).

The animator starts up the round with questions like: how did I feel during this session? When did I feel particularly good? At what moment did I feel tense, nervous, discouraged, saddened?

After all those who wish to have expressed themselves, the animator (progressively, this will be a child) can reflect faithfully on what each one has said, without adding any comments. A prayer or a moment of silence can conclude and open this part of the session.

When we take a longer time for the re-reading, the animator may ask questions which will facilitate a sense of awareness: what has changed amongst ourselves since the beginning of the year? What are our common grounds? What are our differences? When do you have the feeling that we have experienced great moments of communion? How can we still make progress? Who would like to see some changes?

4. Interaction games (getting-acquainted games, cooperation games, etc.) are good ways of making the system of relationships evolve.

THE SOCIOGRAM

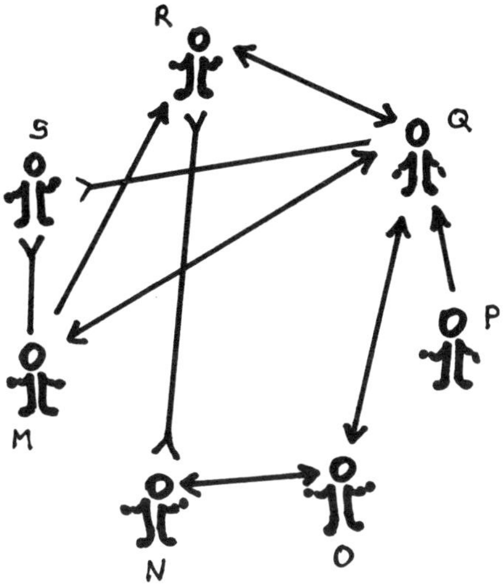

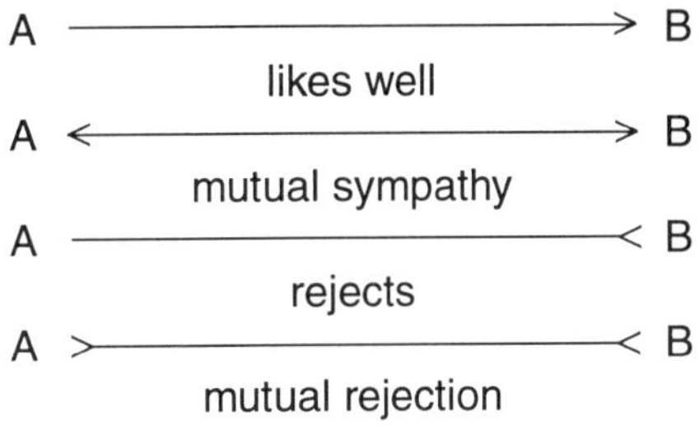

Who is leader? isolated? rejected?
Is there a subgroup?

Everything can change very quickly with children. However well it is set up, the sociogram will reflect only one moment. But constants can also appear. We suggest that you set it up empirically, from your observations, altering it as need be. (To set it up more technically, you must question the children about their preferences, something that is not always indicated.)

The session journal

Date	Mary	Veronica	Dominic	Francis
8 Feb.	criticized Peter's drawing	took the initiative to read	was always looking in Veronica's direction	encouraged Thomas dared to sing alone
	took a place beside Francis	interrupted Mary three times		
15 Feb.	no pep, looked preoccupied	tried to cheer up Mary	interrupted me several times with questions	told Peter 'You're not the one giving orders here!'

You can re-read your journal, your personal files and your relationship cards as you do the Bible, in a prayerful way...

3. A group pursues objectives of action

By 'action', we mean here the tasks and the explicit goals for which the group has come together: we are a group of catechesis, or a football team, or an organized movement. We want to accomplish something together, not just anything. That is what motivates us.

The common action is translated by concrete, easily identifiable objectives, which interconnect among themselves to trace an itinerary:

Year objective:	We are in September. Next June, we will invite our parents and friends to COMMUNICATE to them what we will have DISCOVERED ABOUT JESUS CHRIST.
Stage objective:	'By putting ourselves in the shoes of Jesus' disciples' during Lent, we are preparing ourselves to LIVE THE PASCHAL EVE IN TRUTH (renewal of the baptismal promises).
Session objective:	We are living a GAME OF ROLE-PLAYING: right after the Transfiguration, the Apostles are discussing among themselves about the question preying on their minds: 'Just who is this Jesus we are following?'

In this area of action, the specific task of the group, we draw your attention to two responsibilities of the animator:

1. HE LEADS the group towards the objectives. He knows where he is going, how to get there and with what resources. He guides and directs.

2. HE MAKES THE CHILDREN RESPONSIBLE: progressively, he leaves more initiatives up to them in the realization and in decisions, without ceasing to sustain and accompany them.

We propose the use of three tools for your task as animator: a new use of the 'session journal' (previous page), an outline of work (see opposite page), a procedure to re-read the realizations (see opposite page).

Using the 'Session Journal'

Go back to the previous page. In the journal (which you surely have written up after the sessions, before you had time to forget), note in a special way (colour, underline) the behaviour of each child in the tasks of the group (realizations, initiatives, successes, etc.). That will help you to stimulate and make each child progress according to his potential.

Work outline (also useful for evaluation)

Prepare yourself for the following tasks and ask yourself from time to time how you have fulfilled them.

1. Formulate objectives that are clear and practical, that can be pin-pointed:
   for the year
   for a sequence
   for a session.
2. Propose an objective to the children: in a motivating way
   by yielding some room (gradually)
   to negotiation and initiative.
3. Leading the journey: by finding GOOD PROCEDURES;
   by preparing the MATERIAL and RESOURCES;
   by giving CLEAR GUIDELINES;
   by encouraging the CHILDREN'S INITIATIVES.
4. Guiding the re-reading (cf below).

Re-reading the accomplishments

We propose to you a simple and effective procedure. To be put into effect according to a variable pace (for example, each trimester, or after each outstanding phase). It completes very well the re-reading of the relationships previously indicated.

- Form a circle around a very large sheet of paper on which you have distributed the names of the children.
- Invite the children to write beside the name of each of the others what successes they have had, what they have done, and accomplished... great or small things... Make it clear that the more they find, the better... You may introduce this with Luke 21:1-4, or read this text after... This game is played in silence...
- You can participate in this game yourself, for example, by noting the accomplishments of a child overlooked by the others... (you have, therefore, prepared yourself to do that, for example, by re-reading your session journal).
- Allow each one to speak: to read out loud what is written beside his name (... you may applaud...), add something no one has noticed, mention what he is the most proud about...

Variations: Use only the spoken word (not paper); ask each one what he has done and others complete; interview each other (preferably with a tape recorder); examine the objects realized, the photos taken at the time of an outstanding event for the group, etc.

4. A group creates its own language and rites

This reality appears to us to be very important for religious education. Indeed, by directing your attention to the language and rites of the children in your group, you may obtain two complementary results:

1. You will know the children better and you will learn their language.
2. You will see better how you can teach them the language and the rites of the Church.

In short, you will experience at your level 'the missionary dynamics of inculturation'; entering into the 'world of communication' of the other so that you may express Jesus Christ in a way that can be understood.

Here is a certain number of codes used by children:

- they have a 'tribe language' with favourite expressions, passwords, 'secret idioms';
- There are also signs of acknowledgement and belonging: clothes, emblems, badges, gestures (way of shaking hands, for example);
- there may be 'tests' to undergo to become part of the group, to be recognized;
- there may be rites of integration, of exclusion, of promotion...

While taking all that into account, do not hesitate to suggest, to invent with the children of your group, some rites and signs, some rhythms and atmospheres proper to your meeting: timetable, welcome and greetings, ways of bidding goodbye, use of first names, group song or dance, etc.

Appropriation

1. Recall your childhood or your adolescence... Do you rediscover in yourself some of the realities mentioned above?... If so, recall very precisely the words, the objects, the rites, the tests... and what you felt in all that...
2. Prepare a sheet of paper on which you will note all that you will hear and observe in your group of children, about language, signs and rites...
3. On another sheet of paper, note a few typical elements of your own language, of your favourite expressions, of the religious language you use, of the signs and rites you propose in catechesis.
4. As a team of catechists, answer the following question: Is there a possible connection between the religious languages and rites and the spontaneous languages and rites of the children? How?

Give importance to the languages and rites that come up in your group!

5. A group obeys rules and adopts laws

Here again, we urge you to pinpoint the norms and laws children spontaneously give themselves: sometimes in a very explicit way ('we have no right to do that...'), sometimes in an implicit way (everyone obeys So-and-so without anyone ever saying he is the Leader). Knowing these laws, you will be able to make them evolve or change more easily 'from within'.

But we would especially like to suggest that you clearly propose rules to the children for this particular group which is the catechesis group. In the list below, we invite you to choose, complete, restate, taking into account what you are, your experience and your group. Be very conscious of what appears to you to be necessary (therefore not negotiable) or useful (and negotiable).

1. Everyone has equal rights and duties.
2. It is forbidden to strike and humiliate anyone.
3. Each one helps others to succeed.
4. Everyone has the right to be heard without being interrupted.
5. We consider our differences as opportunities and not as obstacles. It is, therefore, forbidden to make fun of anyone who thinks or acts in ways different from mine.
6. If I have something against anyone, I will tell him first.
7. In order to arrive at a decision together, everyone must be heard. What has been decided in this way by all must be respected by all.
8. If anyone transgresses a rule of the group, he must make amends.

This is a good opportunity to present to the children the sense of the law as a means and an expression of communion, of covenant, in view of a life project (which is both a promise and a grace of God, and man's response).

On the occasion of re-readings, at the end of a trimester, for example, it will also be useful to revise the laws of the group, its rules of the game: certain points must be made more explicit or concrete, others must be modified, still others must be added. Every time that this is possible, texts from the Gospels will be used, for example, some may be drawn from the 'Sermon on the Mount' (Mt 5-7 or again Mt 18: the way of living in community according to the gospel).

Appropriation

In order to give full dimension to the adoption of a law by a catechetical group, we could not recommend too strongly that you 'study in depth' the Biblical theme of the Covenant. Ask a competent person (animator, priest, biblical scholar) to help you set the 'law' within this context.

According to the state of mind of your group, you could, after that, consider a 'celebration of the Covenant' with a proclamation of the law and a commitment to respect it (provided this be done in an atmosphere of joy and freedom).

6. A group evolves and lives a whole history

Like people, groups have a history. In the wake of studies, now considered to be classics (Tuckmann), people admit that this history goes through four typical phases which we summarize in the chart on the opposite page. It is useful to know them, so as not to lose heart in phase 2: a period of crisis is normal and useful.

We add here a fifth phase which appears important to us because it is, par excellence, the moment of re-reading and openness. In this last stage, the animator will take care to incite the group to appropriate its own history for itself. Naturally, it is much richer than the 'typical events' of the four phases. He will also help to experience positively the 'death of the group' and the openness of each towards what is still to come.

The essential initiative to make this transition is:

The re-reading of the experience

We have already presented an initiative of re-reading about the relational and affective experience (see p. 92). The re-reading of the experience is subjected to the same rules: freedom of expression, attentive listening, restatements, syntheses.

The role of the animator consists especially in: motivating, letting others speak, assuring they will be heard, eliciting the synthesis.

Without neglecting the affective and relational level, the re-reading of the experience is more global. Its aim is to reconstruct the history of the group, such as it is perceived by the children, through outstanding facts, a movement, a progression, interruptions and advances made (individual or collective).

The re-reading is extremely formative for it allows children to appropriate their history by telling it. It opens the future by the living memory it makes of the past. It is important to educate the children gradually to discern the common aspects of their history and the differentiated personal aspects: everything did not necessarily mean the same thing to everyone. Through this tension between what is 'mine', what is 'yours', what is 'his or hers' and what is 'ours', the child will learn to affirm himself, to find his place and communicate without merging with the group.

Finally, re-reading is a biblical process par excellence since the whole Bible is, in short, a re-reading in faith of the events of the past in order to direct the future. A re-reading in phase 5 is a new chapter of the Acts of the Apostles in the process of being written.

In practical terms, the re-reading can be expressed by : the word (oral or written), drawing, mime, song, dance, image... It can be the object of a communication, a prayer or a celebration.

Far from being limited to the past, the re-reading commemorates in order to launch life again into a project.

What is going on	In order that everything may go well, the animator may... at the level of RELATIONSHIPS	at the level of ACTION
1. *Group shapes itself* (Forming) Curiosity... prudent restraint ... anxiety... somewhat rigid... cf the first day of school	Greeting each one warmly... putting at ease... by one's way of being, immediately set a style, a spirit... Suggest getting-acquainted games...	Making secure by means of clear information concerning the objectives... precise guidelines... Excellent preparation...
2. *There are tensions!* (Storming) Confrontations... struggles to know who gives orders... or to play a particular role... conflicts of opinion... resistance to norms...	Allowing conflicts to be expressed... while assuring a sense of security!... Helping each one find his place and his territory, urging to respect those of others.	Refocusing on the action objectives... Setting up activities of cooperation... Thinking of the leisure activities and those which release tensions...
3. *The group structures itself* (Norming) Conflicts are resolved... balances and compromises are sought... communication is more open... laws are born... an atmosphere...	Giving importance to signs of cohesion... ambience... Discreetly promoting the integration of the isolated or the rejected...	Formalizing and negotiating a law of the group (cf p. 101) Giving more responsibility and initiative...
4. *Cruising speed!* (Performing) Each one now has his recognized place... The positions and roles are more flexible... an openness to the 'outside' is beginning.	Encouraging each one to be himself, to progress in his line...Inviting to communicate and share with the otside	Allowing the children to have the maximum of initiative... supervising all the while... Animating less by directing and more by inspiring...
5. *The song of farewells* (Bye, bye)	Proposing and animating the RE-READING and the CELEBRATION (with the mission!)	

27. The Bible in catechesis

Do you understand what you are reading? Acts 8:30

You know this from experience and our first chapters reminded you of this: the Bible is at the heart of the catechetical initiative. All the textbooks and all the approved itineraries are centred on the Word of God. This is true, more or less. But the fact remains that, today, no more catechesis is done unless it is biblical, at least in intent.

On the other hand, methods to read and 'work' through the Bible are many, varied and interesting. We refer you to specialized works for that and we draw your attention on the points that appear fundamental to us.

Catechesis aims therefore at developing understanding of the mystery of Christ in the light of God's Word, so that the whole of a person's humanity is impregnated by that word. CT 20

The opposite page illustrates this strong statement made by John Paul II, suggesting meanwhile a few ways of realizing each of the four objectives represented by the illustrations. The following chapter will deal in greater depth with the question: how can the Word and experience be linked in a vital way? For the moment, let us content ourselves with bringing out in the open the biblical initiatives which are inadequate in catechesis:

(a) a simple study of the Bible, even if it is well directed, achieves only in part, or even not at all, the goal of catechesis which is the impregnation of the whole of man's personality, according to the words of John Paul II; it can, to be sure, contribute to it;

(b) likewise, we cannot be satisfied with calling upon the Bible to come to our rescue to illustrate or justify a point of doctrine or pre-established morality.

We could never insist too strongly on the importance of your biblical training and we urge you to complete it.

Appropriation

1. Examine attentively the drawings on the opposite page. For each stage, make the inventory of the methods and the means you know which could be adapted to this stage. Share them within the framework of your team.
2. Find out about the possibilities of biblical training existing in your region. See the list to find out if there is something useful to you.
3. Why should you not decide, as a team, to offer yourselves some biblical training? Whom could you call on? If you do not know anyone, who could give you some information?
4. Reread closely the catechesis textbook that you use, and see, in the light of the opposite page, if it offers all the characteristics of a good biblical initiative. If not, it is up to you to supplement it. Find out how to do this as a team.

Offering the Word...

Presenting the Book
Reading
Narrating
Explaining.

... it is the Word of God!

The liturgical and respectful approach of the Book (candle, incense, bowing, 'dramatizing' 2 Kings 22...) Offering a Bible within the context of a celebration.

'... so that the whole of a person's humanity is impregnated...'

... it is good for the heart!

Interiorizing, meditating
Reading slowly with music
Chanting, singing, praying.

... it is written for us!

We, the children, can communicate with this Book, enter into it, do something with it, play in order to understand better...

Can an ancient text vitalize my experience? How?

> What kind of book makes a difference in one's life? A book that, for the reader, constitutes an 'experience of truth'. (...) It is a book that reveals us and gives form to a truth, ignored, hidden, profound, formless, that we were carrying in ourselves. (...) Such a book leads us to the discovery of another truth, strange at the outset, which joins our truth, blends with it and becomes our truth.
>
> Edgar Morin, *Le Temps stratégique*, No 26, 1988
> (quarterly review, Geneva)

The Bible is the account of a history, an experience. Through people committed in the innermost depths of themselves, at the level of their vital questions.

Thus, beyond the text, there is an experienced history. Events, to be sure, but grasped from within by people who felt touched and who asked themselves: Why?

The Bible relates experiences felt to be particularly outstanding and decisive by those who lived them. Experiences of faith: encounter with God, with oneself, committing and renewing, on the whole, relationships with others and with the cosmos.

These texts were acknowledged by Israel and then by the Church as authentic testimonies, possessing a universal value, of encounters with the true God, the Only One. Inspired texts.

Before the text, there is the reader, myself, us. Through the mediation of the text, I come in touch with the experience that gave rise to it. It is true that this experience occurred in circumstances far different from the ones in which I find myself. But I discover that other human beings – we have this humanity in common! – were touched in a way meaningful to me, that they asked themselves questions similar to mine. Distanced in time, we find ourselves close in the experience.

Among ourselves, the text is used as a mediation, a connection. An inspiring text. But without any automatic response: the fold of the book is the symbol of a dividing line, that of my free decision.

Note for the enthusiasts of hermeneutics (= art, science of interpretation):

According to P. Gisel, we would readily say that an interpretation of the Bible is 'exact' inasmuch as there is equivalence between, on the one hand, the relation between the written word to the experience which produced it, and, on the other hand, the relation between the commentary (theological, hermeneutic) on this word and the experience here and now (structural homology). According to our diagram: if P2 is to E2 what P1 is to E1. As Catholics, we would add that the Church magisterium is qualified to judge the validity of the doctrinal interpretations. Cf P. Gisel, Vérité et Histoire, pp. 273-274; 603 and ff, Beauchesne/Labor and Fides 1977.

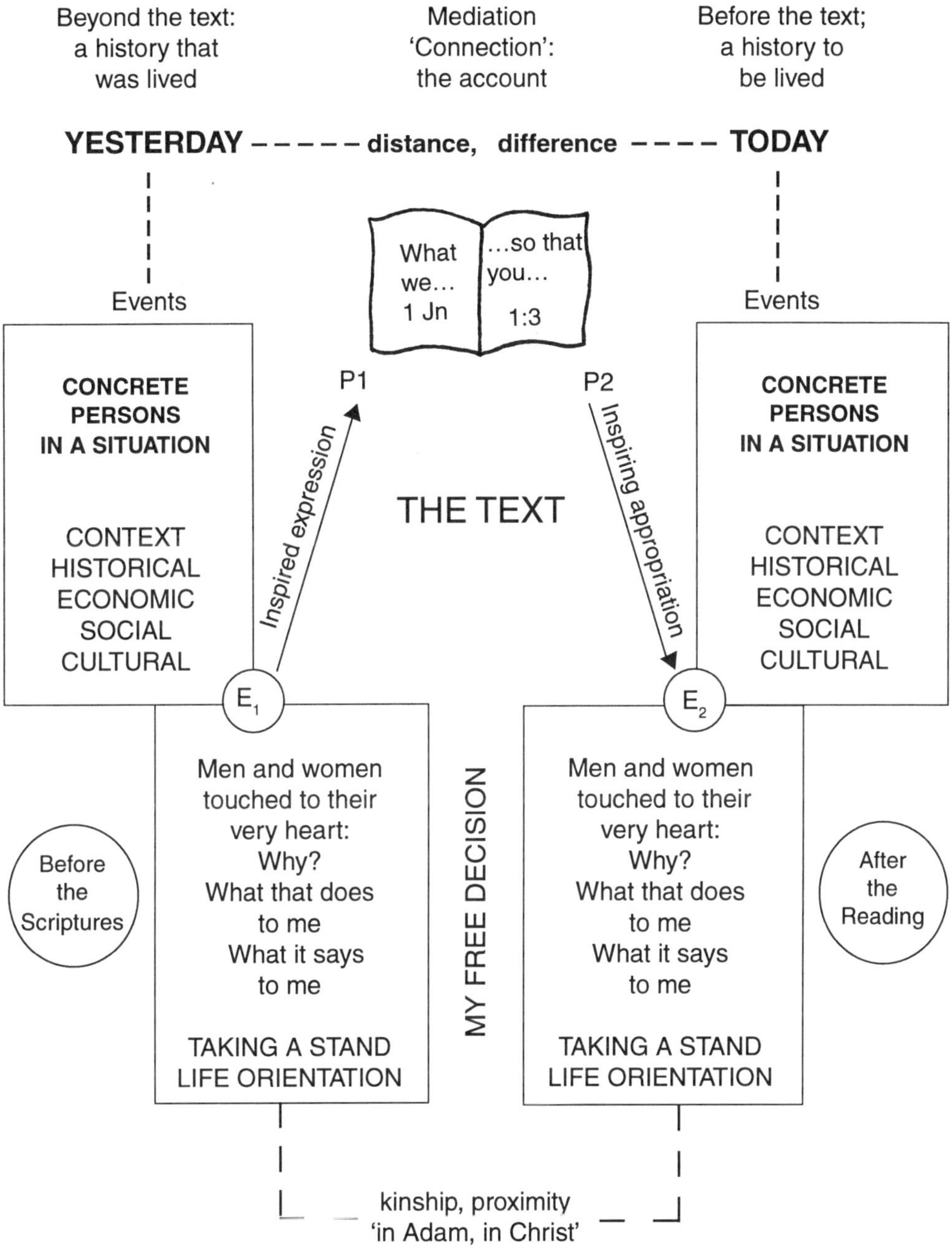

P1 = Written word
P2 = Word interpreting the text
E1 and E2 = Experience in a situation

28. Correlation

Were not our hearts burning within us while he was talking to us on the road, while he was opening the scriptures to us? Luke 24:32

Two men on their way. They have experienced an **event** which has overwhelmed them. In the depth of this **experience**, one question: why? for what purpose? Someone joins them in their experience and their questioning. He opens for them these Scriptures they already knew but of which they had not understood the **meaning**. And behold! Scripture for them becomes the **Word** that changes everything: the heart is aflame and their vision is different. They have had the experience of the encounter with Christ, they can now **live in faith**.

In this story of Emmaus (Lk 24), we are told how man and God meet: through the vital contact between a human experience and a Word understood with faith. That is what we call CORRELATION or setting up a profound relationship between 'LIFE' and 'FAITH'. There lies the most decisive stakes of catechesis. And of existence.

But before speaking of catechesis, it seems to be useful for us to set the correlation in a more general perspective. Indeed, the same applies to correlation as to any faith experience: it is rooted in a human experience, a 'secular one', which must be taken into account. Under pain of no longer understanding anything about faith...

The words in bold in the first paragraph are the key words that will open us to the understanding of this phenomenon of correlation which is so important (and fascinating!).

1. Correlation, a process of human development

To live is a unique experience, proper to each one of us. But each one builds and directs his own and unique experience in contacts made with others. This is an obvious point that each one can verify on his own all through his existence. Education during childhood and youth is the most spectacular illustration of this.

Appropriation

Before going any further, we propose that you make a list of all the elements of response you can find to the question: how can the experience of others help me build up my own? By what secret paths of different experiences can they communicate with each other and even communicate themselves? These are elements of responses present in your mind... and also in the previous chapters. Look for them and note them...

Two preliminary convictions form the basis of the idea of correlation:

1. Man is a being, capable
   - → of knowing
   - and
   - → of loving

Man is CONSCIOUS.
He can perceive himself and find his place in reality.

He wants to understand and give MEANING to his life.

Man can COMMUNICATE and COMMUNICATE HIMSELF.

Human beings CAN MAKE THEMSELVES PRESENT to one another in a vital exchange of COMMUNION.

2. Man is an incomplete being. He is called (by Someone?) to participate in his own creation. He is challenged to be, freely, the author of his self. His thirst, 'whetted' to know and love, turns him to the other, to others... to the Other.

It is really this incompleteness of man and this capacity he has of participating in his own fulfilment that provides a basis to the idea of correlation as a transmission of experience. Indeed, whereas the animal is programmed by its instinct, man is referred back to his fellow humans in order to build himself. Where would he find, if not there, points of reference and models to guide himself? Through the complex game of imitation (which is more than simply copy) and of identification (not to be confused with alienation), man invents himself by taking nourishment from the experience of others. Whereas an animal species is a system closed in on itself by the programme imposed by instinct, we can see humanity (in its totality) as an open system of communication of experience. Correlation constitutes a specific approach, within the overall phenomenon of communication.

CORRELATION IN GENERAL

IS...

WHAT?		**HOW?**		**WHY?**
Making the EXPERIENCE of others (individual or communal) my own	▶	**Through MEDIATIONS**	▶	**Freely fulfilling myself in my power to know and to love**

EXPERIENCE???

In whatever I live, there is the event level and the experience level. It is the same reality but lived at a different depth. The event is what happens to me. The experience is what it does or says to me. The event is still the exterior reality. Experience is what I understand and what I become through what happens to me.

Human experience has the character of a history. Through some experiences, we live one experience, that of being brought into the world. A gripping history in which there is the interplay of our 'happiness', 'our salvation'.

EXPERIENCE

Something happens to me...
I do something...
Something is done to me...

EVENT

That DOES something TO ME... **I feel** an emotion... **I am touched** affectively in my identity and in my relationships.

That TELLS ME something... I seek to understand... **I search** for a meaning... **I ask: why?**

LIFE PROJECT
My story in History

Example:

In a precise situation, someone strikes me on the face... ... that 'does' and 'tells' me very different things according to who strikes me and why... an impaired stranger... or my colleague seeking to humiliate me in public...

In apparently similar events... ... very different experiences!

Appropriation

1. Find three events, great or small, which happened to you recently. Recall precisely the event (what happened). Ask yourself: what experience did I live there? What did that do to me (affectivity)? What did it tell me (meaning)?
2. Share with your team. Practise identifying your experiences.

A mediation serves as an intermediary, a bridge spanning two realities between which there would otherwise be no communication. Between two human minds or two human 'hearts', **the first and most fundamental mediation is the living and speaking body**. But what can be used as mediation to link two beings through space and time as a whole?

According to the American sociologist Peter Berger, on whom we are relying here, man and society, in some way, mutually produce each other. Man produces society and society produces the man. That is realized in three movements:

- Man constantly expresses his inner activity in actions, productions, creations. By doing that, he fulfils himself and brings himself into the world. This is exteriorization.
- The PRODUCTS of human activity become a reality external to man, which imposes itself upon him and acts in him. This is objectification. We call these products of human activity cultural MEDIATIONS: language, documents, tools, works of art, machines, etc.
- 'Interiorization is the reappropriation by men of this same reality.'

Let us express things in another way. Through exteriorization, men express their EXPERIENCE in works (documents and productions of all sorts). These works are then available as cultural MEDIATIONS. By coming into contact with them, other men can appropriate for themselves the experience of which they are the expression. That is how men very distant in time or in space can communicate with others and communicate themselves.

An example. The famous icon of the Trinity by Roublev is a mediation. It is the fruit of a faith experience which has exteriorized itself in it. Centuries separate me from Roublev, about whom I know almost nothing. Nevertheless, by an attentive contact with the icon, in some way, I appropriate for myself his experience. I make it my own. His experience can awaken and nourish mine. Our two experiences remain different – one is his, one is mine – but one is born from the acceptance of the other. It is the same for everything we call 'culture', in the broadest sense of the word (which allows us to develop our experience).

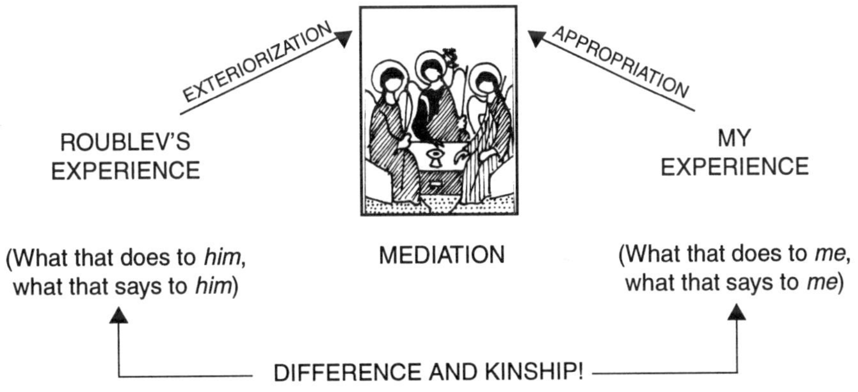

Correlation is to establish a relation between two or several experiences through mediations which function as elements of a language.

CORRELATION???

To sum up, we can say that correlation is this process by which my experience is nourished, in some way, from the experience of others, through the intermediary of an object or of a document serving as mediation. What is at stake in correlation is not negligible since it is a matter of communication at the deepest level, that of the experience. And having no limits in time or space!

We can now describe in a more precise way the stages of the **process of correlation.**

1. It all begins by the **contact with a mediation**.	I meet someone. I read a text. I admire an object.
2. I enter into an **active relationship with the mediation**. I try to decipher the message left in it by someone else. I try to make out the experience 'behind it'.	I talk with the person. I analyze the text or work of art. I am attentive to everything that 'makes sense'. I read someone's character. I discover the experience of another.
3. **I appropriate for myself** (or not) **something of the message** given by the mediation. I build **my experience** in this way.	I become aware of what that does to me (affectivity) and of what it tells me (meaning). I place myself in relation to 'that': by integrating it (or not) into my experience, into my system of representation and sense (KNOWING) and into my affective dynamism (LOVING).

Comments

1. The three stages are necessary, but there is truly correlation only in the third.
2. Making a correlation in someone else's place is impossible. I cannot say what that does to him and what that tells him. I can still less decide how he wants to position himself in relation to 'that'.
3. But we can correlate with someone. By deciphering the same mediation. By sharing what that does to each of us: we will perhaps discover that we are similar, perhaps different, probably a little of both at the same time. And that is very enriching. That is called communion in difference. (Already, that can be like God... the Trinity, don't you think?...)

Note on AUTHORITY

Correlation is essentially a free and individual initiative. No one can do it for someone else. What then about authority? Is it not within its power to impose a meaning and even a decision? We are not thinking here of political or military power but of moral authority. In no way do freedom and authority exclude each other. I can freely acknowledge that particular persons or particular instances have a particular authority to interpret certain messages:

- either because they are the very author of the message or else its privileged witness;
- or because they possess a skill allowing them to decipher effectively the message which objectively exists in the mediation (a connoisseur of Picasso will help me understand his works);
- or because they have profoundly integrated the message (someone who has lived intensely the experience of compassion will be in a position to help me understand all the messages dealing with compassion).

Authority thus imposes itself upon me as the necessary reference. It speaks to me in an authorized way. But it cannot – even it! – speak in my place. In the face of authority, I remain responsible. And my first responsibility is perhaps to make a good choice of the one whose authority I will freely acknowledge, in what domain and in relation to what criteria. My own and free choice then commits me to take account of that authority.

Contrary to a blind and infantile submission, there is a mature acknowledgement of the authority which liberates one from narrow-minded subjectivism.

Note on the COMMUNITY

If the experience is unique and personal, it is also communal. Far from isolating each in his subjectivity, it opens out to the community:

- the MEDIATIONS have a collective dimension. Either because they are the fruit of a common experience, or because they have been effected in a human, social and cultural context;
- SHARING EXPERIENCES (correlating with and in a group) is already a communion experience (differences enrich each other and connect together in a collective history).

Appropriation

As a team, choose a clipping from a newspaper (this is a mediation), for example, relating an incident for which you feel concerned, because it deals with ecology, non-violence, AIDS, justice... Go through the three stages of the previous page... Become aware of the difference between the second and the third... Examine how your ways of reacting come together and are differentiated... how the exchange has enriched you or has been a problem for you... in whom you acknowledge an authority on this matter and why... That's it, you have done some correlation!

2. Correlation for a Christian

Correlation is a way of putting human experiences in vital communication. We would now like to outline what that means for a Christian, by setting the correlation within a theological perspective.

1. **Caught up in the correlation, the fulfilled man is the divinized man.**

God's project, the key to the whole of history, is to introduce man into the communion (co-relation) of the trinitarian Love.

The Fathers of the Church used bold statements to express this 'mad' project (so brilliant it is). May these be 'mediations' for us!

> The Word of God became man so that you may learn from a man how man can become God.
>
> St Clement of Alexandria
> *Protrepticus*, 8

> He became man so that we could become God.
>
> St Athanasius
> *The Incarnation of the Word*, 54

> God wants to make you God... through gift and adoption.
>
> St Augustine
> *Sermon* 166

> The Word became man so that man might be bound to God.
>
> St Irenaeus
> *Adversus omnes Haereses* II, 18, 7

2. **The original and perfect realization of this project is Jesus Christ**

In Jesus, humanity and divinity are in a co-relationship in a way of particular interest to us. Between the humanity of Jesus, indeed, and his divinity, there is perfect unity: he is the same and unique person. But there is also a distinction, a certain ' dynamic tension', clearly visible in Gethsemane ('my will – your will').

The Council of Chalcedon expressed this by saying that, in Jesus, the human and the divine are united 'without confusion nor separation'.

This is what will be analogically realized in our divinization: we will be united to God without confusion nor separation. We will be ourselves, he will be himself, but we will be one in him in love.

Here is another way of saying the same thing.

Bruce Ritter is an American priest, founder of the Covenant Houses which welcome young people, victims of prostitution and organized crime. This text is a meditation that communicates his experience to us... and that of God.

'That there be babies, fine! But that God became a baby in order to be absolutely like us, that would surprise me. That would mean that we can love him as a person and that he, too, loves us as a person. You're joking!

'We are in the process of going beyond bounds. It is better for us to keep to the hypothesis that Jesus was a man so perfect that he was like God. If I say that, the Church will jump!

'Well, let us say that Jesus was God and that he was like a man. He possibly had a real body or an unreal body, or an ectoplasm. Or that was possibly only an illusion. But the Church will still be shocked if I say that. All the same, no one would still make me believe that God had armpits and all the rest.

'That would mean that the Trinity is not satisfied with its host of angels and that it wants to be with us? The Son would thus become Jesus – or the opposite – because he loves us? Do the three Persons love us to that? Obviously, it is easier to love like us and whom we can touch. But the incarnation cannot be something that simple. Yet, the Church says that it can. In short, where lies the interest?

More precisely, why did one of these Persons become a man like us? I am well aware that we have problems, but still... So that we might become like it? Strange. It is true that at Christmastime, it is easier for us to love one another. The three Persons, as far as they are concerned, do nothing but love each other all the time. Perfectly! In other words, if we act as they do, and love one another all the time, we are like them. That means that we are made in their image and in their likeness. Wow!'

Bruce Ritter,
La Maison d'alliance, p. 235, Fayard 1988.

3. Revelation, or how God communicates his experience to us

For some, the word Revelation evokes a set of truths, of formulas, a knowledge about God and the faith. In a word, a doctrine. The consequence: they think that by transmitting this knowledge, they transmit the Revelation. A dangerous illusion from which we, in catechesis, must keep away. Not that the transmission of knowledge does not have its place, much to the contrary, but this transmission is meaningful only within an experience that carries it and makes it explicit.

For that is what Revelation is: the communication of an experience, that of salvation, an encounter with the living God who gives life.

God did not transmit to us 'truths about himself'. He transmitted himself.

> Revelation is the personal gift God makes of himself.
>
> Karl Rahner,
> *Traité fondamental de la foi*, p. 199.
> Le Centurion 1983

> Knowledge of God is an *experience* of God...
> God can be authentically approached only in an experience of relationship... The trait proper to love is not to define itself in an abstract way, but to manifest itself concretely.
>
> André Dartigues,
> *La Révélation*,
> pp. 151, 152, 157.

That is why Revelation is a history, the history of the encounters with God, and not an accumulation of facts.

'I am the God of your father, the God of Abraham, the God of Isaac, ... the God of Jacob', God said to Moses (Ex 3:6). We know God only if we communicate with the experience of those who had an experience of him. It is to that God that Jesus refers (Mk 12:26). That is the God of whom he communicates to us the vital knowledge, that is the experience. Cf the boxed text quoted in chapter 2 (p. 22).

Appropriation

1. From this Christian view of Revelation, draw a few consequences for catechesis. Note them and check them with others.
2. As a team, and from what you have learned so far, tell one another how you understand this statement: in catechesis, correlation puts knowledge at the service of the faith.

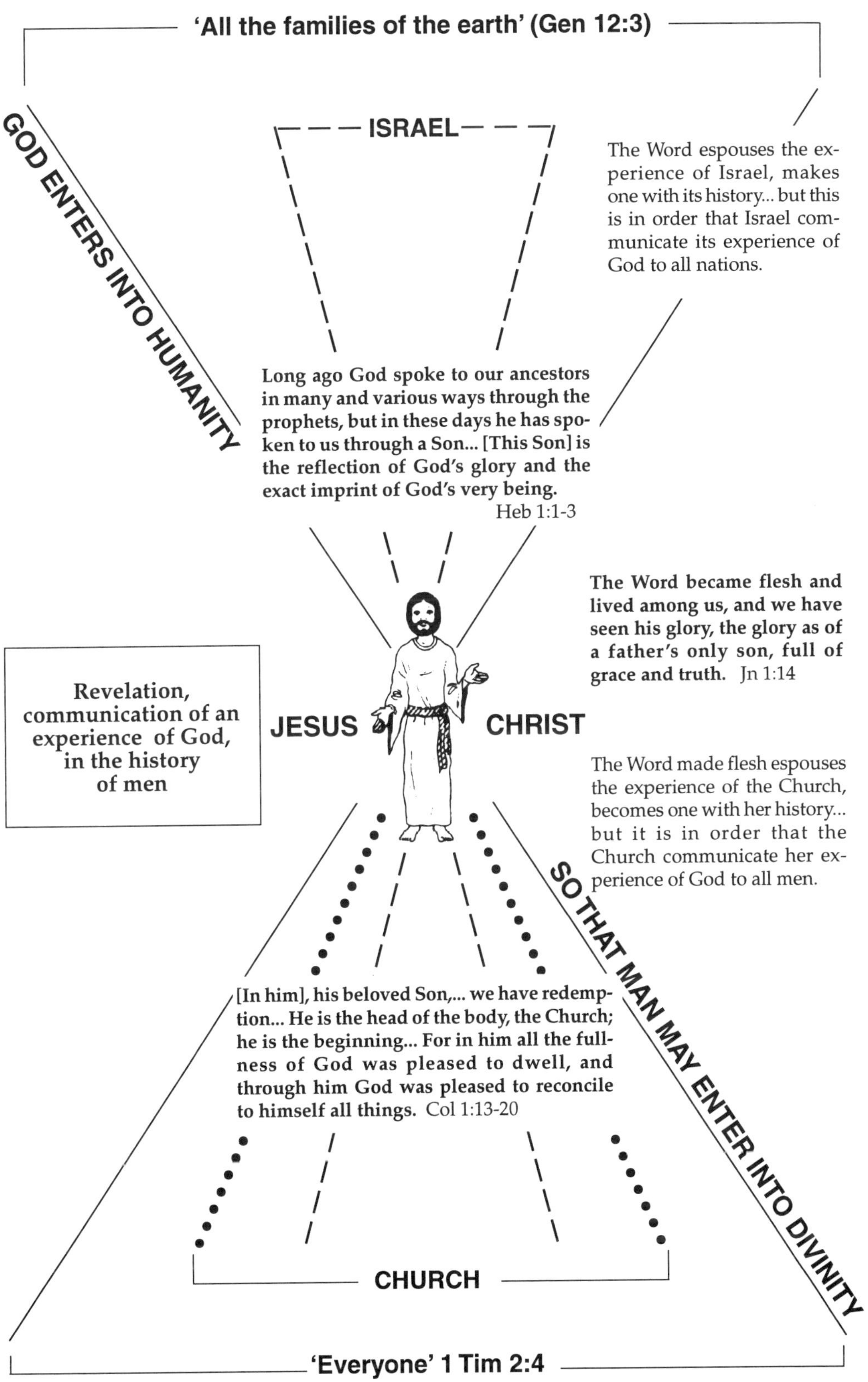
'All the families of the earth' (Gen 12:3)
GOD ENTERS INTO HUMANITY
ISRAEL
The Word espouses the experience of Israel, makes one with its history... but this is in order that Israel communicate its experience of God to all nations.
Long ago God spoke to our ancestors in many and various ways through the prophets, but in these days he has spoken to us through a Son... [This Son] is the reflection of God's glory and the exact imprint of God's very being. Heb 1:1-3
The Word became flesh and lived among us, and we have seen his glory, the glory as of a father's only son, full of grace and truth. Jn 1:14
Revelation, communication of an experience of God, in the history of men
JESUS
CHRIST
The Word made flesh espouses the experience of the Church, becomes one with her history... but it is in order that the Church communicate her experience of God to all men.
SO THAT MAN MAY ENTER INTO DIVINITY
[In him], his beloved Son,... we have redemption... He is the head of the body, the Church; he is the beginning... For in him all the fullness of God was pleased to dwell, and through him God was pleased to reconcile to himself all things. Col 1:13-20
CHURCH
'Everyone' 1 Tim 2:4

3. Correlation in catechesis

In the light of what has been seen, we can now find a place for correlation in catechesis.

its AIM: It merges with that of catechesis and we can go back to the words of John Paul II: 'The definitive aim of catechesis is to put people not only in touch but in communion, in intimacy with Jesus Christ.' CT 5

Correlation proposes an appropriation of the experience of Christ by the child. In this way, it aims at a free identification with Jesus Christ.

its REALIZATION: Correlation pursues this aim by proposing to the child to link what he lives (in EVENTS) with Jesus Christ (communicated by the Church MEDIATIONS), in such a way that his EXPERIENCE may become a FAITH EXPERIENCE.

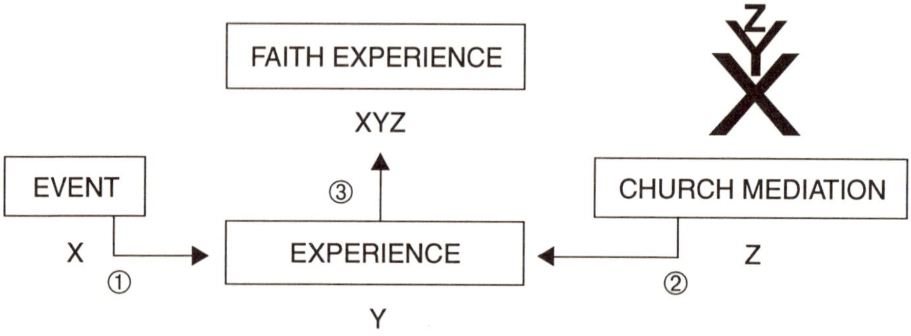

In the first movement (1), the child passes from the event to the experience: in what happens to him, in what he lives, he becomes aware of the effect it has on him (affectivity) and of what it tells him (meaning).

In the second movement (2), the child personally appropriates for himself the experience of Christ or of the Church, such as he has perceived it through a mediation (Bible or other).

He can then choose, freely and consciously, to live his own experience in faith (3).

Appropriation

Read or re-read GCD 74. Compare with what we call correlation.

Surely, you can easily see that correlation is not:

▶ *a simple superficial contact with a mediation*

for example
- looking for an 'example' in life to illustrate a truth of faith;
- a quotation from the Bible to justify a 'lesson' of good behaviour;

▶ *a simple intellectual deciphering of the message of a mediation*

for example
- accumulating biblical facts as pure information of which the child does not see the vital link with his experience;

▶ *a simple statement of the official interpretation that the Church has given of her experience through theological formulas.*

for example
- memorizing definitions and 'answers' of the catechism;
- knowing what 'the Church thinks'.

All that is not devoid of use and value but it does not achieve the goal proposed by correlation. The nature of correlation expresses itself through a new star!

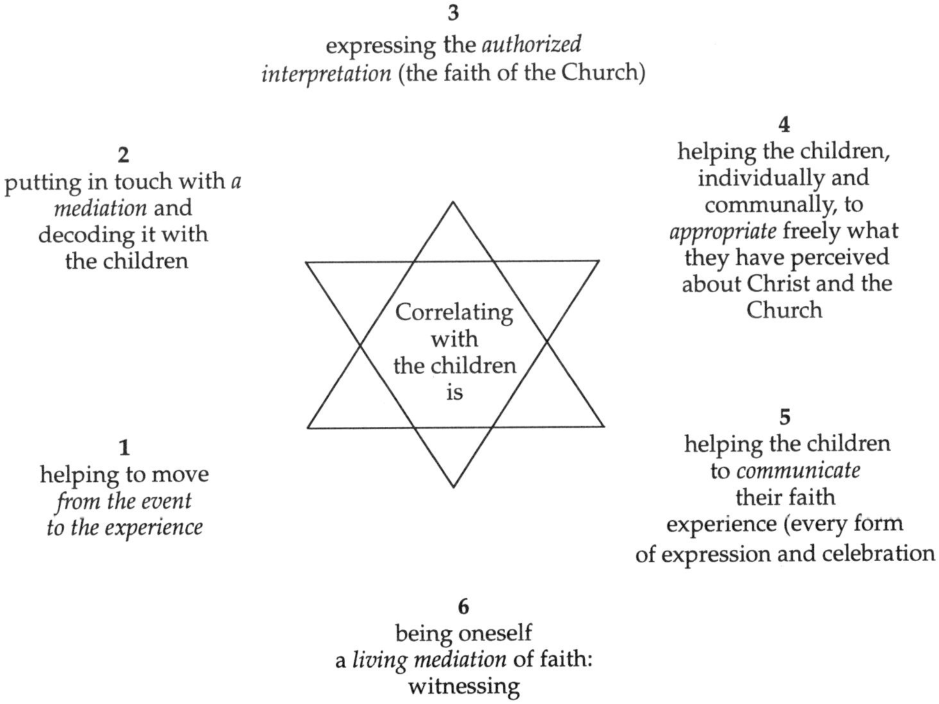

Correlation and Christian community

Correlation always has both an individual and a communal dimension (cf p. 109). In catechesis, we will particularly see to it that:

- the collective dimension of the events and the message given by the mediation be taken into account;
- the different interpretations and expressions of experience be allowed to express themselves and be connected together: among the children themselves, between the children and the catechist, between all of them and the Church authority.

This task is not always easy: at the beginning, each one (including the catechist) is tempted to impose his experience and his interpretation, or again to be satisfied with a superficial agreement to avoid any 'conflict'. But, progressively, all can develop the capacity to hold both ends of the chain: to differentiate and affirm themselves, while seeking the points of convergence. They then commit themselves to a process of communion in truth. It is a conversion and a liberation. A rich and fascinating experience.

Correlation and Church authority (the Catholic point of view)

Please refer back to page 109 (Note on authority). For a Catholic, the first type of authority lies in the Episcopal College in union with the Bishop of Rome. The second type of authority may be attributed to the theologians, the exegetes, as well as to other experts in human sciences. The third type of authority is proper to canonized saints and to all Christians who live authentically from Jesus Christ.

The authority of the catechist

The catechist himself may enjoy the three types of authority. By virtue of his mission, acknowledged by the bishop, he can speak in the name of the Church. By virtue of his formation – we hope it is as thorough as possible – he has the necessary competence to decode the Christian message. By virtue of his living faith in Jesus Christ, of his love for him, he can be a witness.

But authority also means the capacity to authorize. To authorize, in the strong sense of the word, is to make one an author. It is to give someone the 'permission' (the 'Father-mission', in French, the 'Päre-mission'...) to become the author of his own life (or its co-author... 'the very Spirit bearing witness with our spirit...' Rom 8:14-16). To have authority in this sense is to allow the child to speak, to awaken his awareness to the rich nature of his own experience, to invite him and give him the means of making it his own at the contact of stimulating mediations. And all that also can be learned (again a reason to form oneself!).

Authority is much more and much better than to avoid the uproar in a group... it is to help them grow!

This first overall view is illustrated and commented in the following pages.

4. Methodology of correlation
Plan for a practical itinerary

Whoever has studied the map of the itinerary carefully will discover a thousand paths in the land.

A wanderer's proverb

A question on meaning is posed

route A

A 1 by an *event*

A 2 where the children feel they are *concerned.*

A 3 This event takes on a consistent reality

A 4 It can lead to an *experience*

A 5 which may be enriched by confronting it with *other experiences,* grasped through *mediations.*

route B

B 1 by contact with a Church *mediation* (The Bible or other)

B 2 which is interesting to *decode* in order to grasp its *message.*

B 3 What does this message *tell me today*? (and the message becomes Word).

B 4 The Word *refers me back to my life*, to *events* I have lived or am living.

Integration/Appropriation

C 1 What do I *understand* better today?
How was the initial question enlightened? shifted? deepened? modified? resolved?
What can I do, what can I be now, after I have followed this path? Towards a *new vision* and a new *orientation.*

C 2 *Communication and/or celebration of the discovered novelty.*

Whatever be the route chosen, A or B, the important point is to follow the whole itinerary indicated by the arrows!

Do not let yourself be tempted to take a shortcut. Go back again through the diagonal which will lead you more surely to your goal; the appropriation and the experience of faith.

A STRIKING EXAMPLE

Here is an example of a concrete journey. We have chosen to follow 'route A'. We suggest that you yourself imagine the itinerary of 'route B'. Thus you will enter concretely into the understanding of the correlation.

A 1

Stages	Good questions	Good means
Event 'I was beaten up by Peter and Nicholas.' (Francis)	(a) Did this really happen to Franciis, a member of the group? He spoke of this spontaneously last week... (b) The catechist is the one who drew up the programme of reflection on this type of event. In this case, how should it be introduced?	'Approaching' an event: taken from a fact which occurred in the group – a spontaneous account from a child – bringing up the event, for example, a cooperation game (never bring out the negative) – strong image(s) representing the event – an imaginary story – childhood memory related by the catechist.

A 2

All those concerned	How should they all be motivated and interested? Reflecting on an incident interests me: – when I have experienced it – when I feel that this could happen to me – when someone close to me has experienced and been touched by it. I participate all the more actively now that I have understood the benefit I will draw from it (what use this will be to me). To feel free is a source of motivation. I can be 'blocked' in respect to a particular event.	– Ask: 'Recall... did that ever happen to you'? Allow time to recall the memory... eventually: relaxing, music, noting, drawing... – Explain the use of this, for example 'to learn to overcome difficult situations... to resolve conflict ...' – Let them be free to become, or not, involved. It happens that a child who, apparently, 'is not with it', is really very attentive... Respect the possibilities of each one to get involved (it is their life) while stimulating them.

A 3

A consistent reality	What realities do they live? The reality of an event is what we have seen, heard, touched, felt... colours, sounds, sensations... To submit our-selves to the trial of reality is the beginning of truth.	– Giving the account in a real and imagined manner. – Ask questions: what did you see? – Make an inquiry (reconstruction of the facts). – Role play.

A 4

Setting for a possible experience	How did they live a particular event within themselves? How do they live it now? What awareness do they already have? What is revealed about their system of representations (about themselves, about life, about the world...)? How can you allow the expression of both the individual experience of each and of what is possibly common to all? How can you provide progressively a language which would facilitate awareness? A good listening experience allows each to be himself... and the experiences to be articulated in diversity and convergence.	Ask two 'good questions': – What did this (or does this) do to you? Level of emotions, of affectivity... Observe the vocabulary in order to sharpen this awareness... – What did (or does) that tell you? Level of understanding, of interpretation, of representations... Allow time for the memory. Non-verbal activities of expression can help: drawing, painting... When the time comes for verbal expression, two golden rules: – allow the freedom to express oneself – assure attentive listening (cf p. 89).

The pages you are reading can be used as a plan to prepare and evaluate your initiatives of correlation. As you do this, you will probably modify the present outline by improving and adapting it to your needs.

A 5	**Enriching ourselves by confronting other experiences**	This stage was already begun in the previous one (confrontation within the group). Are there any other interesting or significant experiences? By what mediations can they be reached?	– an interview or inquiry outside the group. – A mini coverage. – Watch a video or an audiovisual montage. – Listen to a song giving an intense message. – Analyze some documents. – Invite someone who can witness.
B 1	**A Church mediation**	This stage can follow, precede or replace the previous one. What mediation should be chosen? A biblical text? A picture (the iconography is rich)? Another 'document of the faith'?	In our example ('I was beaten up'), one of the three following texts could be chosen (each having the effects of different meanings): Mt 27:30: the children are invited to identify themselves (role-playing, for example) with spectators who are asking themselves questions… Lk 23:33-43: idem. Jn 18:10-23: the children could be in the shoes of Jesus' guard.
B 2	**Decoding the message of this mediation**	What means could you put to work: – so that the children be active? – so that the operation of decoding be fruitful? – and so that we may not always be doing the same thing?	See especially the means suggested in the *box of tools for biblical animation* and in the works describing some techniques of animation. In the other example, that could be: – a role-playing game – a 'bibliodrama' – a discussion – a textual analysis done from a plan.

B 3	**In this message, what Word is there for me today?**	How to help children enter into a more personal context with the message? How to foster interior listening?	– Making silence – Meditating – Each one expressing himself in his own way – Making the character with whom we have identified ourselves speak.
B 4	**This Word refers me back to my life**	In the case of 'route A' chosen in our example, we step over this stage which was given at the beginning. Similarly, if we were in 'route B', we would perhaps step over stage A5, inasmuch as we would judge it to have already been given at the beginning (B 1).	
C 1	**Integration Appropriation**	Prepared by B3, this stage leads further, in the sense that here is where the child really effects his correlation. How to stimulate him and give him means of appropriation?	Asking good questions. As in our example: – You were beaten up and so was Jesus: What does that do to you? What does that tell you? – Could you say what Jesus said to the guard (Jn 18:23) to the one who beat you up? What would you say to him? – Do you want to forgive him in your heart? Can you? Allow time for reflection, for meditative silence… The child can answer this in his head or in writing or…
C 2	**Communicating Celebrating**	Often, the best way of appropriating something for oneself is to communicate it. Moreover, that reinforces communication. And that allows for re-readings…	All the means of expression: speaking, miming, symbolizing… **Attention**! It is the expression of faith of the children. With their convictions and intuitions, already Catholic, but also with their questions, doubts and resistances…

5. A summing-up chart and a verification scale

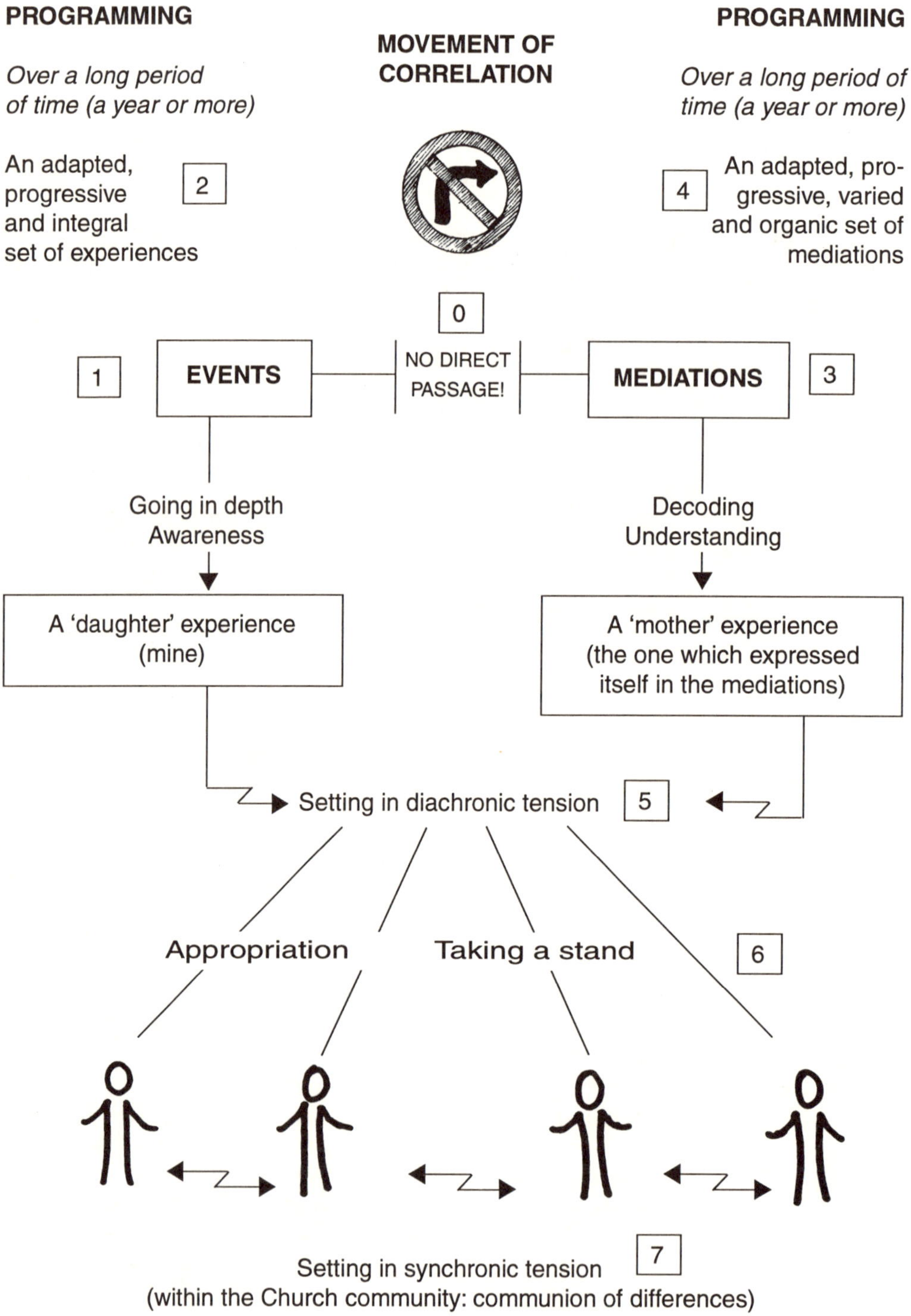

Seven questions plus one!

The chart on the previous page can be used as a verification scale. Here is a brief commentary on the questions we should ask ourselves to evaluate our catecheses from the point of view of correlation.

0 Do we carefully avoid the pitfall of the direct passage from the event to the message of the mediation (or vice versa)? *Otherwise, we are working hotchpotch or superficial moralism.*

1 Are we concerned about proposing ways of moving from the event to the experience (going in depth, questioning, becoming aware)? *Otherwise, we are staying at the anecdotal stage of life.*

2 Over a long period of time, do we take into account a coherent, adapted and relatively complete set of experiences? For example, the lights and shadows of life, the individual and the relational, etc. *Otherwise, we risk evangelizing only a part of the being.*

3 Are we concerned, through the mediations, about reaching the experience at their initial sources (the work of decoding and understanding)? *Otherwise, we risk projecting our preconceived ideas on these mediations.*

4 Over a long period of time, do we offer contact with an adapted, coherent and relatively complete set of mediations in a way that allows us to be captivated, along with the children, by the whole Revelation? For example, by drawing as much from the accounts of miracles and parables as from the liturgy, from testimonies of success and of misfortune... *Otherwise, we risk being partial and give the children only that which we ourselves think we have grasped from Revelation.*

5 Do we allow the emergence and the maintenance of a good tension between the 'mother' or founding experience (which is expressed in the mediation) and the 'daughter' experience, that of today? In respect for the historical (diachronic) distance. This tension implies a resemblance (a kinship of experience) but also a confrontation, somewhat like Jacob's wrestling (Gen 32:25-26). The encounter with the Word is a hand-to-hand struggle in which agreement is disputed against resistance. Let us not be afraid of questions and doubts. *Otherwise, we run the risk of being satisfied with superficial, fleeting allegiances.*

6 Do we give space and means to the work of appropriation and to a personal stand? *Otherwise, our initiative could well be reduced to an abstract reasoning exercising no real impact.*

7 Within the group of catechesis, are we concerned about letting the dynamic tension between the various stands taken by the children, between theirs and ours, between ours and that of the Church magisterium (setting up synchronic tension) express themselves? A tension implying both setting up a relation and distancing, confrontation and communion. *Otherwise, it is to be feared that we remain at the level of deceitful unanimities, of a poor hotchpotch of opinions.*

29. The family: The first initiation into spiritual life

A few pages **for you, parents,** in this work on the formation of catechists. Why?

– Because we both have the same objective: the full happiness of your children!

And then, in catechesis, the family appears as the first 'catechetical setting'.

In chapter 13, we wrote that the home is the shaping hearth of the child's first experiences. We will come back to this a little later.

It is also a matter of transparency. You will have a better understanding about what goes on in catechesis. You will develop a liking for it, if that has not already happened long ago. You will judge better how earnest we are in our attempts to initiate your children into the encounter with Jesus Christ in the Church.

– Finally, by everything that comes out of your heart, you constantly tell us how and to what extent one can love what one creates. By your life as parents, in spite of mishaps or deviances, you illustrate one of the great truths of our faith: the creative fatherhood of God.

Besides, Jesus himself has chosen you to be an image of his Father: 'Is there anyone among you who, if your child asks for bread, will give a stone? Or if the child asks for a fish, will give a snake? If you then, who are evil, know how to give good gifts to your children, how much more will your Father in heaven give good things to those who ask him!' (Mt 7:9-11).

Thus, we are at ease with you, as we hope you are with us because of your children, the first adults of the year 2000!

Here is the plan of this chapter:

1. In the form of an account, and in connection with powerful moments for catechesis, we shall tell you again that YOU ARE TOUCHING THE ORIGINS OF LIFE.

2. Under the title DISCERNMENTS, we will offer you three keys to a spiritual education.

3. Between a 'good morning' and a 'good evening', a brief itinerary into the three words from the heart will urge you to conclude with us:

TO CELEBRATE
IS TO FREQUENT OUR FUTURE

N.B. Deliberately, we will not speak of God in these chapters, except in slight allusions, to remind you of the raison d'ètre of this work.

You are at liberty to read here an experience of faith or again an experience of life in faith!

1. You are touching the origins of life

Certain biologists reduce you to being the simple bearers of the germs of the human species. They attribute such power to a spermatozoid and an ovule, that they start from them to explain the story of your love.

There is some truth there. Science says that nothing suits an ovule better than a spermatozoid, and vice versa. 'Boys are for girls and girls are for boys,' sang Jacques Brel.

Our own knowledge tells us that, if for a male there can exist all the females of the world, for a man who is truly man, there are already far fewer women; for a woman who is truly woman, there are already far fewer men!

And when FRANCIS met BERNADETTE!!! They sought each other in what they had unique in the world and irreplaceable. The story of their freedom began to stand out: each became meaningful to the other.

Oh! that was not without turmoil: fervours, crises, waits, projects. In short, one day they noticed that wherever Francis was truest to himself, there was Bernadette; and wherever Bernadette was truest to herself, there was Francis. They needed each other to be who they are. One had begun to suffer or rejoice in the heart of the other. For the first time, they were going to give the dimension of their whole life to their freedom. They became husband and wife!

You know? – They have never seen the love they have for each other! They recognize it by a whole network of signs they give each other, like an invention: glances, smiles, kisses, embraces, tender love. They tell each other words, not at all scientific, but so full of sense, which are truer than science: they love each other. And when, sometimes, there are no more signs, life is worse than a desert!

Their bodies... that is where they express themselves and read their love.

Their bodies, that is the place for their language, their very own language, and themselves at the same time: 'I love you'.

There, in the nest woven by their relationship, come one... two... several children into this world. The nest is sometimes so powerfully fruitful that it calls little ones to enter into it, with the heart alone! That is called adopting... Francis and Bernadette, at the origin of three children.

Every time they are worried and astonished, they admire what they have managed to do... with one tiny seed and a garden that gives itself.

Attention: the apartment is full, the end of the months longer.
Worries, fevers... the big one who... the little one who...

But, above all, do not touch it! It would be less serious to go for the parents!

I love you < the two of us < that is they.

Time should be taken to listen to life being lived...
what you are, what you live, what happens to you
appears fascinating to us.

- Being at the origin of human lives. That each child, boy or girl, benefits from the humanity of his father and of his mother. Not only of one or the other, but of both, together.

- Being a father, a mother, long before the child becomes aware of that. A reality, a truth in which he is invited to bring in 'd... d... daddy... m... m... mummy'! What did you not do to make him recognize you and show it!

- And you remain parents, whatever the way the child will accept or reject your fatherhood or your motherhood, whatever pride or shame he will experience for himself or in front of others. So it is. And since you are at the origin, it is up to your own truth as well as to his own to share it with him, because it is beautiful, and very simply because... it is!

  Whether the child denies you, whether he may want to take your place instead of keeping to his own, that does not change this first reality and truth.

  Yes, that may hurt, very much; one can die from that.

- The arrival of a little brother or sister, when the child learns to say a 'you' other than to his parents. Another 'you', but similar!

  You know the problem very well: the 'you' to the brother, to the sister, it must often be said to please Daddy or Mummy, and the 'me' benefits-in-the-loss... difficult to translate even into daily life!

  But, when we manage to do so, it is cause for a celebration, because, there, we rise again from the past and the future becomes a promise again.

- And the meals! You remember the first time your child was promoted to your table: you wanted it to be with you, even if at the beginning... All the same, you did not make that up in order to be able to tell him someday: 'Now, to bed without your supper!'?

When the whole family is gathered around the same table, each child in union with the same source, acknowledging that each of the others has his place, all that, born of you, tells you again: it was good for you to have taken the risk of this love venture.

'THANK YOU,
DADDY AND MUMMY,
FOR HAVING DONE ALL THAT FOR US.'

When they say that, who are the happiest ones?

2. Discernments

Education poses a question. It is not improvised. We do not have to treat this subject. We are simply setting up three milestones, to set the companionship of the growth within the life of relationships and within spiritual life.

First discernment

> There are two spontaneities: that of instincts
> that of love.
> The first preserves, the other creates.

No doubt you cannot explain why you love each other. The ultimate reason, the true one, remains a mystery. You would have to tell your whole story. And again: why him?... why her?...

Perhaps you are there to respond with your whole life!

And if death comes to play havoc, it is because you love each other. 'To love' means: I want you to live. I want it so much that I would give my life to tell you that.

With the children, why so much love?... often misunderstood. At the time of a preparation for baptism, a father was confiding to the group of parents: 'The way I love that kid is real madness! The other day, I said to myself: my father's love for me was the same. Yes! And I had to have a child of my own... – finally myself, excuse me: the two of us! – to discover that. I had seen nothing of this!' His own father could not get over the fact that his son called him to say: 'Thank you, Dad!'

Your own children, why do you love them?

- The more beautiful ones? the more obedient? the more grateful?

You love them all, and none in the same way. Could it be that they need your love so much because they are from you? The most reticent of children consumes more of this love and receives more: the supreme justice of love.

Your way of loving is like that of God!
He does not love us because we are lovable,
he loves us because he is good.
His love creates goodness in us.
He makes us beautiful with all the love he gives us!

At the beginning of the life you received to give, Someone loves your children and has chosen you to reveal this love to them, you... the first ones!

Second discernment

> Even with all the authority in the world
> I cannot manage
> to make an oak out of a grain of wheat.

At least, that is evident, you say!
Happy parents...
Blessed are the children for having prophetic parents!

Yet this is no trap. It is a discernment problem: how do we recognize a grain of wheat?

– The grain of wheat and the acorn, that is easy. For the children, it is altogether something else: they do not really know, there is no label on them!

There we have a first fact: we do not know.

So, we do not act as if we knew! And already, you note a first economy: we do not base our authority on ignorance: all the more lost!

Can we know? Our little Paul, what is he?

– A daisy? a carnation? a tulip? a wild rose? a buttercup? a rose?
– A rose!

The problem is that almost all parents give birth to roses. And there are many men and women who play the rose game because the other flowers, apparently, are not so beautiful...

They remain buds all their lives, without fragrance. They make others believe that roses have thorns, whereas in reality, the thorns have the roses!

What a mess: they would have made such beautiful carnations...

Discernment:

...a rose, is that our wish
or else
is that what our child is?

We love our child (first discernment),
We are attentive. We listen, we watch, we are patient.
We talk about him among ourselves.

Uncle Henry is the one who solemnly asks him one day:

– And you, little Paul, what do you want to be when you grow up?
– A policeman!
– Wouldn't you rather be this... or that?

You are already learning something: uncle Henry would not like to have a nephew be a policeman. That does not help you much, but you keep that in your heart: policeman.

Discernment:

... What does he mean by that?

– At least, a policeman is not like a punk. The uniform that leaps to the eye? The traffic cop who directs the cars?...

There is an immense tenderness in this creative wait of the parents.

And what an exercise!

– General... he received a military tank.
– Locomotive driver... he plays with an electric train.
– Taxi driver... he would so like to drive his father's car.
– Pastor... he attended his cousin's baptism: a beautiful ceremony.

In short, we are giving you these few very simple examples and, in the same line of thought, we are illustrating the approach that tries to discern the what-is-to-come in the what-is of the child.

But little Paul will never say that he wants to be a man, and God knows how your heart is set on the hope that he will be one!

Same discernment: following the child while making him out, listening to him living in order to see the directions he is taking.

Indeed, there is a first obedience which provides the true ground for the authority of the parents. It is the attention to what is 'growing' in your child, to what he is intimately and to what he, too, is seeking, as he faces things and people.

Listen to him live and you will not trace his path: you will search for it along with him!

Thus you will keep on being father and mother in his story.

There, you can lead him with authority.

Authority does not mean: first, to command,
it means to increase, to foster growth.

With all the authority in the world, you will not manage to change a grain of wheat into an oak tree. But what a power you hold, like the sun and the water, and also like the plough at the proper time, to prepare the harvest of the stock of wheat!

Creators... with God?

Third discernment

> There is a way of life that stifles
> and a kind of death that makes one live.

No growth without crises!

It is not only the clothes that become too small when a child grows. Clothes are external: we can put on other clothes.

Here, it is the same one who becomes another: he loses his feathers in the process.

So, you know that; your child crosses over to new stages of his history.

Now, in the spontaneity of love, with an authority that makes one grow, you discover that overcoming each crisis implies a certain death for your child. Until he has assumed these deaths in his own personality, you can be present. He will experience them through the welcome you give him every time, on the new landing he has reached. Otherwise, he risks taking refuge in the situation he was in 'prior to his death', because there he was at peace; or of ruining everything in the rejection... of taking the paths of neurosis or anarchy.

Two examples:

- the first, an inner process of maturing, like the bud opening out;
- the second, an external demand, like a challenge.

1. The child moves from the 'he': 'carry, Daddy!... drink, Mummy!' to the 'me', 'I want'. You know that this is the moment when many fathers wonder what they might have done to God to have such a child: headstrong, a character, and, if we do not cater to his whims, he howls when he does not go into a tantrum!

At the moment you are reading these lines, the crisis has passed for quite some time; but you have grasped what is at stake for the next crises.

Our whole life implies these 'deaths' that the acceptance and the presence of a friend help us through.

The little devil is not a devil: he is finding out that he is a subject. He is becoming aware of this wonder and poses as such. And more often than not, by imitating the king, his daddy, who is allowed to do everything, and he: nothing!

To listen to this child living, and to love this child, is to reach him up to that point, and to help him come into this world as a little person, to help him make his first steps toward freedom, in your home, because that is also his home.

At the same time that the child becomes able to love, he has an experience of love with his parents. He enters into a relationship.

2. Obeying... that is difficult because, somewhere, it makes you die.

'What's all this mess in your room? Hurry up and tidy it!'

'The tragedy is that the "mess" for my mother is my own "tidiness"! I feel good in my own world. When my mother tells me to tidy up, it means I have to throw everything into their box which they have placed in my world. My idea of tidiness does not exist for them. Her tidiness, that's everything!

And who gives in every time? I do... in order to have supper!

No! this time, I'll have my own way...'

And Mom is the one who tidies up because Dad is coming.

Indeed, there again, the child must die to his well-being to please his mother. Sometimes that works: when the love for the mother in the child's heart is stronger than his own pleasure.

If the relationship is fine, everybody will be happy, even Daddy, when he comes in.

BUT

If there is a breakdown in the relationship? If there is a refusal, a tantrum and yelling?

It is precisely through this kind of S.O.S. that the child is giving signs of these deaths which bring him out into a new light. These new aspects of existence are generators of anguish for him, because he has not given them any meaning yet.

Let us let him speak:

Mummy, do you know what you are asking me?
I don't yet know how to tell you.
You, you should know so well.
But I no longer know if you are looking at my heart.
So, come and hug me, so that I may know how to please you.
Some day you'll see, I will be able to do all that all by myself!

Thus, in discernment, love becomes creative, authority fruitful. The wings of the child open out. He dares launch himself: if he falls, he does so in your arms.

...Three discernments...

Concretely, they lay the foundations of education, not on the fatherly and motherly instinct, but on the gift of self, on what we have called the spontaneity of love. They take into account the original factors of life and growth. They put their stakes on the quality of the relationship which unites the parents to the child and invite the child to respond to them in his own name.

At once, this relationship gives the child the space and time to structure himself at the beginning of his history: it allows him to die to his crises and come out of them without leaving unpleasant tastes and seething feelings in suspension to poison his whole existence. It opens to freedom, to autonomy; it increases the capacity to enter into oneself within this relationship, to trust. It prepares peacemakers and a new quality of life to be transmitted.

Christian education is not added on to that education, it places it in the hands of our Father who is God: it holds it from him!

3. Three words on earth to listen to heaven

Please... thank you!

It is mealtime. The children are seated at the table. Daddy takes his place, from which all the other places are determined. Mum brings in the soup. Peter is starved: 'some bread!'... louder: 'some bread!' Mum serves the soup. Peter: 'some bread!!!' Mum:

'Some bread, if...?

– **If you please**.

– If you please, whom?

– If you please, Mum!'

And Peter is given a nice piece of bread he brings to his mouth. Mom takes the bread again. Peter:

'Thank you.

– Thank you, whom?

– Thank you, Mum!'

... Peter eats his bliss.

Thus, a stomach affair has become an affair of the heart! Yet, the bread was there: parents know what their children need. Why ask? Why say thank you? That is useless. Perhaps. But it changes everything: a mother, a father are acknowledged as other than servants: a son consciously takes his place within the relationship that makes him live. We are light-years away from a lesson on politeness.

Do you know of a better initiation into the personal prayer of petition and thanksgiving?

Forgiveness!

That's it: a breakdown. So little is needed to hurt a heart, when it loves. There is never any breakdown in indifference: no one is there. And the breakdown leads to panic, because the heart of the child no longer knows where to turn. An enormous difference from what the parents feel. They know from experience that much is learned from the mistakes that are disciplined.

But if they do not discern that they are actors in the drama being played in the heart of the child, it is difficult for them not to take advantage of the situation. Then they begin by bringing up the mistake. They use phrases to develop a sense of guilt:

– What did you do?
– You're happy, now?
– That's right, all you had to do was to obey!
– God is the one who punished you!

– *I know it all too well.*
– *As if I could be happy!*
– *Is she happy that I did wrong?*
– *He goes about it the wrong way to tell me he is good!*

And suppose the child needed the look of the offended to interpret his mistake... and his **forgiveness**. Because his panic rises precisely from that, because he is not making the distinction between his mistake and his relationship with the offended.

– You love him?

– Tell him so!

Do not say: 'That's nothing.' Depending on your nerves, he has already been slapped, deprived of television, you will tell Daddy! But do not let him dwell in his unhappiness. In a word, follow your heart, not his mistake. And build up a loving heart with him again. You will express your grief as well: we can tell so many things to each other when we are reconciled. And when he learns that it is the same with the Lord, his God, he will feel he is on familiar ground.

Good day! Good evening! Goodnight!

You have never relied on these greetings from your children to spend a good day or a good night! If they say them, if you demand that from them, it is so that THEIR day may be beautiful, THEIR night peaceful.

These little words mean: I know you are with me
I am your child
I am aware that I am loved...

And often, in the evening, this takes the dimension of a real rendezvous. Awaking from, or on the threshold of sleep, there is, so to speak, a birth and a death of the awareness because this is the rhythm of their lives: 'Sufficient unto the day is the evil thereof.' And you are happy for them because of a 'Good day' or a 'Good evening'. In fact, you who know. Don't your little ones make up a beautiful catechesis for you? 'Good day, Lord...' 'Good evening, Lord!' Your morning and evening prayer, that is not for him, it is first of all for you!

> – Rites are necessary.
> – What is a rite? said the little prince.
> – It is also something too forgotten, said the fox. It is what makes a day different from the other days, an hour from the other hours.
>
> Saint-Exupéry, *The Little Prince*

Thus the life of relationships begins to radiate in the family. How could it not be celebrated? It makes us live!

Deep down, you have noticed it: someone who loves does not ask himself why he exists. It is as if, in love, he has his reason to exist.

It is when he no longer loves, or is not loved, that he wonders what he is doing there.

To celebrate the life of relationship is to celebrate the heart of man because that is where he finds **meaning**; that is, his **significance**: sharing, communication, pooling one's resources, communion... and his sense of **direction**: he is already 'becoming familiar' with his destination. He is 'decking his heart' for his future: a heaven of relationships!

You will find that on every page of this work: because the celebration of the heart of man has become, in Jesus Christ, the celebration of the heart of God.

30. A course in religion at school

Apply your mind to instruction and your ear to words of knowledge. Prov 23:12

YES

- It is part of culture.
- How can you understand Dostoyevski without religious culture!
- This is the opportunity to reflect on existential and ethical questions.
- The history of Europe is part of the history of Christianity.
- The stories in the Bible shape our collective imagination.
- The roots of our cultural identity lie in Christian civilization.

NO

- Religion is a private matter.
- Pluralism must be respected: the school must remain neutral in this domain.
- It suffices that a professor of French or history point out the religious dimension of certain questions.
- Religion cannot be learned.
- A stranglehold on the school by the Church must be avoided at all costs.
- 'Christian civilization' no longer exists: let us forget about it.
- A good course in computer science is much more necessary.

N.B. In this chapter, we are considering only religious education, not the properly so-called catechesis which, in certain areas, also exists within the school framework.

After a period of study on the matter, the present tendency in Europe is rather to advocate that a religious culture be maintained or restored in the public school programmes. The arguments most often offered are:

- Threatened to be colonized by the imperatives of the economy, the school must at all costs remain faithful to its humanistic and cultural vocation. Now, the religious fact is a constitutive element of culture.
- Our own history cannot be separated from Christianity. To ignore this is to doom ourselves to become illiterates of civilization.
- Because it poses the ultimate questions of man and his destiny, because it offers a treasury of experience and wisdom, religious culture brings an important contribution to any education wishing to promote the quest of meaning and the structuring of the personal identity.
- It is absolutely possible to effect a religious education that makes the riches of the religious tradition available to everyone, all the while respecting individual consciences and their freedom.

▶ A CAPITAL ASSET
(that is precious!)

- made up of DOCUMENTS and INSTRUMENTS that GENERATIONS HAVE ACCUMULATED through the centuries.

▶ OF MEN
(that is precious!)

- who THIRST
for KNOWLEDGE
for INTERIOR TRANSFORMATION
for DEVELOPMENTS OF THEIR SENSITIVITY
- and are CAPABLE OF USING the assets available to them.

Culture, civilization, these are rather vague terms we can enjoy differentiating or opposing or combining. I shall not dwell on that. As for myself, I have told you, it is a capital asset that is shaped, used and preserved, that grows and declines, like all the capital assets we can imagine – of which the best known is, without doubt, what we call *our body*...

Of what is this capital asset Culture or *Civilization* composed? It is first of all made up of things, material objects – books, charts, instruments, etc. – which have their own probable duration, their fragility, their precariousness of things. But this material is not enough. No more than a gold ingot, a hectare of good land or a machine can be capital assets in the absence of men who need them and know how to use them. Note these two conditions. In order that the material of the culture be an asset, it requires also the existence of men who need it and may use it – that is men who thirst for knowledge and power of interior transformations, who thirst for developments of their sensitivity; and who, on the other hand, know how to acquire or exercise what is necessary in terms of habits, intellectual discipline, conventions and practical uses to utilize the arsenal of documents and instruments that centuries have accumulated.

Paul Valéry, *Regards sur le monde actuel.*
Gallimard.

Appropriation

1. Do the 'pros and cons' exercise on the previous page. Weigh and discuss each argument. Complete as needed.
2. With the help of the key to its reading (see left column), take time to understand the logic of Valéry's text.
3. Do you think that religious culture, or Christian civilization, also offers a specific asset? If so, make an inventory of it: things, documents and instruments which are the legacy of this culture...
4. Do the yearnings and capacities indicated by Valéry also appear to you as directed toward religious culture? Justify your opinion.
5. Compare Valéry's view of things and our presentation of correlation as a process of human growth (pp. 104-109).

Cultural approach to religion

> Thus we can say that religion has played an irreplaceable role in the venture of building a human world. Religion is what allows the furthest self-exteriorization of man, allows him to impose most effectively and completely his own significations on reality. Religion implies that human order is projected. on the universe as a whole. In other words, religion is the boldest endeavour to conceive the entire universe as having a human significance.
>
> Peter Berger, *La Religion dans la conscience moderne*

Religious culture contributes to man's humanization.

N.B. We are using the word CULTURE in its first sense: everything that enriches the mind, sensitivity and experience.

The religious tradition is a true treasury of cultural mediations. The opposite page evokes them. Through contact with these mediations, every man is reached and helped in his effort to understand himself, to take his place in the community of human beings, in the world and in history.

Far from being a threat to individual freedom, an approach of this kind gives freedom its true chances by urging it to exercise itself and take its stand on essential questions.

What difference is there between catechesis and religious culture?

- The catechesis group is a Church setting. The class is a social setting undetermined from the religious point of view.
- Catechesis supposes a faith motivation. The school is founded on the need for knowledge and formation.
- In catechesis, religious documents are given to nourish and mature the faith. At school, they are made available to nourish reflection and personal experience.
- Religious expressions of explicit faith are proper to catechesis: prayer and celebration, profession of faith, testimony in life. Promoting these expressions is not the mission of the school.
- The catechist is a witness of Christ. The teacher is a cultural mediator.
- In catechesis, the Church is the authority (cf p. 116). At school, the Church is not a normative authority except in particular dispositions of the law (public acknowledgement, concordat).

Riches to which everyone has the right: religious mediations

The *Bible*, a monument of universal wisdom.

Elements of response to the ultimate questions: man? God? life?

The treasures of *religious art*, reflections of the mystery of the world (architecture and sculpture, painting, music, literature...).

The experience of the wise and the saints: styles of life which have left their mark on history, initiatives at the service of men, illuminating actions...

Religious *expressions*: prayer, liturgy, symbols and rites.

Key moments in the *history of Christianity*, shadows and light in the opacity of time. In order to have a better understanding of ours.

Appropriation

In each box, note a few realities (objects, characters, events) which, according to you, are part of the universal heritage which ought to be made available to the largest number of people.

SCHOOL pertinence...

> Inasmuch as it is an integral part of the school, the teaching of religion must fully assume the demands and the proper character of the school reality: the serious nature of the programmes, scientific quality, participation in the educative and didactic project of the school, adequate qualifications of the teachers.
>
> Emilio Alberich, *La Catéchèse dans l'Eglise*, p. 231, Cerf 1986.

With regard to the model we described when we spoke of catechesis (chapter 28), we propose a pedagogy of didactic correlation for the school. It is always a matter of an active contact with cultural mediations, drawn from the treasury of the religious tradition, in order to enrich its experience. But, in the context of the school, correlation aims neither at the profession of faith nor the testimony of life.

Didactic correlation

Religious mediations (objects, documents)	question ← A	**The experiences of the children and youth of today.**
Bearers of questionings and meaning, witnesses of experiences of permanent and universal value (even if they rose from situations or from events of the past, as experiences, they are not surpassed).		They experience new situations and events. But the vital questions are not alien to those asked by others elsewhere or in the past.
Perceiving, locating, decoding, understanding, interpreting.	B → to enrich oneself	**To have a better understanding of self, to place oneself within one's personal identity in the community of human beings, in the world, in history.**

As for the catechetical correlation, two routes of programming come up (they may be combined):

- route A organized from key problems or experiences which are proper to a particular age group, to a particular capacity of understanding and, from there, questions the religious mediations;
- route B is organized from the mediations (to be discovered, understood) to lead then to an appropriation (reflection, taking a stand).

The specificity of religious teaching in the school framework, may be made evident on three levels: content, objectives, pedagogy.

CONTENT

It is divided into two areas (which may be combined) that correspond to the two routes mentioned previously.

The religious facts,
in its multiple aspects, perceived through mediations:
- biblical culture
- prayer and liturgy
- artistic expressions
- ethical and historical aspects...

The human experience,
with the traits proper to each age group:
- personal identity, knowledge and development of self
- communication, relationships and social life
- visions of the world, life choices, ethical problems.

OBJECTIVES

1. To inform in a serious, coherent and organic manner
2. To train in understanding and discernment
3. To develop the sense of awareness, of self-affirmation and dialogue.

According to E. Alberich, op. cit., p. 233.

PEDAGOGY

Religious teaching in school may accommodate itself to different temperaments and various pedagogical options. However, it will reach its objectives all the better if the following requirements are honoured:
- taking the two areas of content into account
- concern for the didactic correlation
- active participation of the students
- quality of the pedagogical relationship.

Appropriation

In the elementary school, what, according to you, should be the broad lines a) of the programme of religious teaching; b) of the formation of the teachers?

31. Companionship and catechesis with persons who are handicapped or marginalized

I thank you, Father, because you have hidden these things from the 'wise and the intelligent and have revealed them to infants! Mt 11:25

'A pastoral and catechetical companionship is used with persons who are handicapped in their physical, mental, psychic or social integrity. In our ministry we meet these persons from an early childhood to an advanced age, often up to the time of their death.

To give companionship to them in their life of faith also means to give companionship to the families and the educative milieux with their own form of organization. That forces us to go beyond our own limitations, particularly our denominational ones. Ecumenical reflection and work are one of the riches that handicapped persons challenge us to live.'

Firmin Rudaz and the pastoral team of French Switzerland in specialized milieux.

'First, we set out to express God to them. And that is already something! It makes us "move" since we set out on our way. To tell them about God... But what we then discover most of the time, is that they are the ones who tell us about God – IN ANOTHER WAY.'

'It is impossible to say to the other: God loves you, without telling him: I love you. That is true always and for everyone, but it happens that we cheat on that. We say: God loves you, but without really saying: I love you. With people afflicted with a handicap or with suffering, we cannot cheat, for they are never mistaken about this.'

'We create programmes and celebrations made to measure. The ready- to-wear does not "go over". Then we are the ones who take up the "made to measure". Ready-made in-itiatives cannot be used as such. There we are forced to be creative: another discovery the handicapped give us to live! and that is no small gift...'

'Handicapped people are really an opportunity for us and for our human and Church communities. An opportunity for openness and renewal. This Word of the Gospel we give them, we receive it from them, expressed and lived in another way.'

'The faithful presence of catechists to the children and young people, particularly to those who do not seem to "want it", is a sign of God's discreet fidelity. To be there with them, accepting not to speak of God... is to give them something of the truth of God.'

Appropriation

Go among these marginal people. Listen and, together as a team, tell one another again what you have heard. And what that urges you to live.

Whoever has become involved in a relationship with seriously handicapped persons – with multiple handicaps – has been able to sense the mystery of the person, buried deep in innermost recesses, muzzled by the handicap – and yet there – totally. This is mind staggering![1]

To live a catechesis with the maladjusted is to enter into communication. It is not a teaching, it is first a relationship. It is a matter of living something with them. There is not always an explicit proclamation of the faith. But that does not mean that we can say just anything. Never will the harm that a bad catechesis can do to handicapped people be adequately denounced: it imprisons them further in their anguish and solitude.

Competence is necessary for that. Empiricism and goodwill are not enough. The more difficult the communication, the more demanding the catechesis.

But what may appear to be slow change to some, to me, personally, seems to be richness and love.[2]

1. Periodical *Recherche. Conscience chrétienne et handicap*, 7. Place Saint Irénée, 69005 Lyon.
2. Désiré-Jacques Coll. Narbonne.

Appropriation

We are always tempted to forget or narrow down the 'margin'. We have enlarged it so that you might dwell in it. Did you ever happen to feel somewhat marginalized? Did you meet people who were?... Beside the boxed text above, note names (persons, places), words, deeds and gestures. God knows? Suppose God revealed himself there in another way?

32. The area of methodology

For which of you, intending to build a tower, does not first sit down. Lk 14:28

The seed would sprout and grow, he does not know how. Mk 4:27

Methodology is the study of the processes and techniques by which we put together in a concrete initiative all the aspects of the pedagogical act: intentions, goals, means, etc. It answers the question: in practical terms, how do we go about it?

First, here is the *methodological circle.* It describes the principal movements of the pedagogical activity. The wheel never stops turning nor the car moving forward!

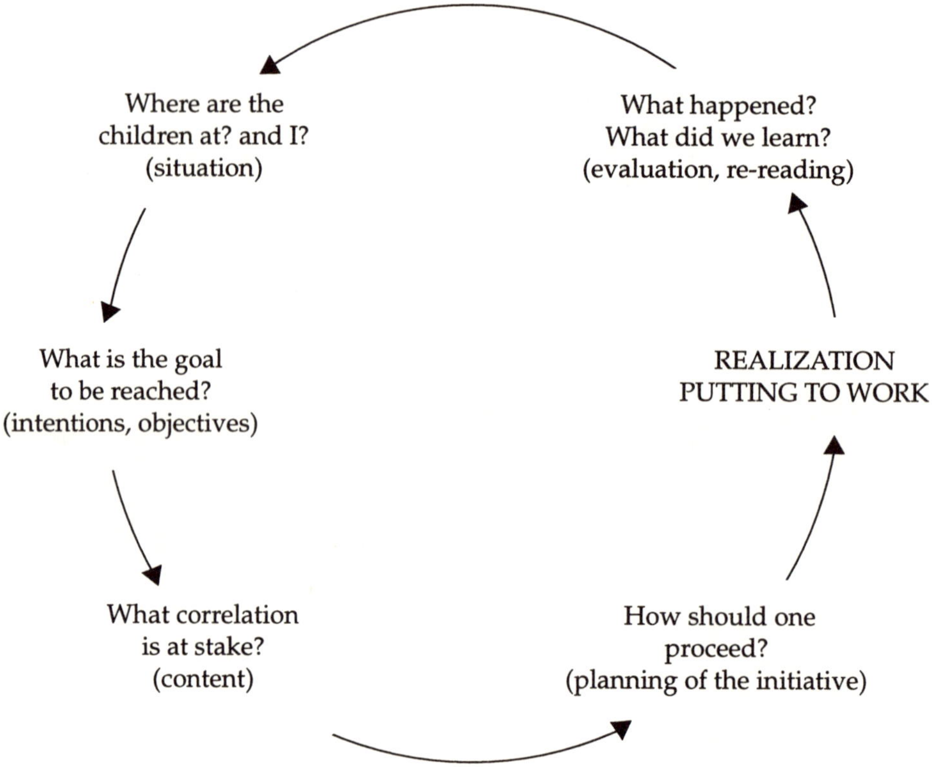

Appropriation

On the theme 'Knowing Christ', make the wheel turn! Imagine what goes on at each stage: make note of some ideas...

And here is the *methodological field*, in other words, the plan of the worksite:

PREPARING

1. **the initiative**	2. **the place and objects**	3. **me**

REALIZING

1. **Greeting** each one personally, in truth: this is not long, but important.

2. **Motivating**: They were 'elsewhere', they must be brought 'here and now'. Awaken the interest for the objective, the learning process, its result.

3. **Learning** (what? why? how?)

Catechist	ACTIVITY	**Children**	**Forms of interaction**	**Resources means**
		KNOWLEDGE:	Summary	Cassette
Proposes Explains Gives guidelines Organizes	Take off	read look listen interpret, etc. Imagine	Work in pairs, in threes, in groups	Invited person Document
Directs		ACTION:	Dialogued summary	Video
Animates Shows Controls Witnesses Relates	Summit	write practise make manipulate, etc.	Debate Round table Role-playing	Slides History objects
Questions Responds Prays, etc.	Landing	COMMUNICATION: talk play meditate, etc.	Personal work Circle Panel, etc.	Notebook or personal file Chart Poster, etc.

4. Completing: – **Consolidate the result by pointing out its value**
(and motivate) – **Take leave personally and warmly.**

EVALUATING

1. **in my head**	2. **with the children**	3. **with the team of adults**	4. **with Him.**

33. Preparation

All your ways will be sure. Prov 4:26

1. Theme – Content – Intention – Objective

Here is the front page of a preparation file given as an example.

Meeting of *15 April 1989*	Group (*Name*) (*11/12 age group*)

Theme: *For us, who is Jesus?*

INTENTION

Knowledge/ awareness	Affective level/interior attitude
Through the 'I am's of John, perceiving the mystery of Christ.	*A special effort for Jesus...*

CONTENT

(Z) **Revelation/ mediations of faith**	(Y) **Experience what that does/says**	(X) **Events in the life of the child**
The mystery of Christ revealed progressively. Particularly, the 'I am's of John (followed by the name of a material object).	*The joy of being 'figured out' without being defined. Figure out the other without defining him. I am more than I can say, so are the others. Fear/sadness/anger(?) of not being figured out.*	*'Verbal caresses': you are a 'dear' a true 'rock'. Invectives: 'rotten seed!' Objects we love, with which we identify ourselves: 'mascots'... 'For Mark, I am a pile of crap' (said by J.)*

Resources: *Gospel of John: 6:35, 48, 51 (BREAD of life from heaven), 8:12 (LIGHT of the world), 10:7, 9 (GATE), 14:6 (WAY) 15:1, 5 (VINESTOCK)*

SEQUENCE	**OBJECTIVE of the encounter**
1. *Game: choose an object that says something about me today.* 2. *Work on the 'I am's of John.* 3. *Apprpriation (link between 1 and 2.*	*Second of the sequence:* *For each 'I am' of John, the children express: what that tells them: (a) about Jesus; (b) about his relationship with us (in writing, personal file).*

Evaluation: Objective reached? If not, why? The unexpected? Elements of re-reading – questions to clarify – follow up?

THEME

This part of the mental world is explored during a certain number of weeks or months. It forms a unit at the level of the intelligence. It provides a conducting thread and a theological problematic question.

INTENTION

The catechist has this in mind as the sight to be aimed at, which he attempts to reach. But he will never be able to assess the result at this level. At the most he will have a few signs. The star is what indicates the direction... but it is in heaven (that is in the soul to soul exchange between God and the child). In order not to remain solely on the cerebral level, we also note the intentions at the affective level of the attitudes we would hope to elicit: hope, trust, gratitude, love, faith, joy, etc. It is important to become aware of these in order to imbue our own way of being and the climate of the meeting (I will not elicit joy by being furious).

CONTENT

These are the elements of correlation on the point of the theme which is the object of the meeting. We try to identify the precise and interlinked aspects: (a) of Revelation; (b) of the experience at stake; (c) of the life of the children grasped through some facts or events.

It is the beginning of correlation that the catechist makes up in his mind. Thus he penetrates into the profound level of experience and faith. At the same time, he prepares himself to help the children to make their own correlation.

RESOURCES

We indicate those which appear to be most appropriate 'to mediate' the intentions and the content.

SEQUENCE

Often, the time allowed for a meeting is too short to live through the phase of a complete correlation. Thus it is of interest to us to conduct the initiatives, in several meetings which form a briefly outlined sequence in the preparation file. Working in sequences assures continuity and progression.

N.B. A textbook or a programme is useful to provide: an overall plan, coherence, progression, suggestions.

OBJECTIVE

It describes in precise and concrete terms (a) the result that the children (b) will have reached (if all goes well!) through this meeting and that the catechist will be able to observe and verify (c). We will always ask ourselves whether the objective is precise and if it can be observed. If the formulation is vague or if 'that is not directly obvious', it is an intention. It must be made more concrete. A beneficial exercise, difficult at first but which 'pays' in the long run and makes people effective and humble. After having gazed at the star (intention), a goal is defined at the ground level... but in the direction of the star.

In relation to the SITUATION OF THESE CHILDREN: where are they at? Where are they starting from?

2. The development

On the reverse side of the *preparation file*, one describes the practical development of the meeting. This outline must be clear, precise and concise. It will be used as a memorandum. On a separate piece of paper, we write some complements like: the essential ideas of a summary, the detailed procedure of a complex exercise. The permanent elements (greeting, leave-taking) are not mentioned, neither are obvious points.

The file speaks for itself. Let us emphasize a few points.

- The first column is not wide: the animator has done the bulk of his work ahead of time, in the preparation. During the meeting, his activity is quantitatively reduced: it is up to the children to play the game! But qualitatively, it remains decisive: introducing little but knowingly and precisely; being present to the children and facing the unexpected.
- The second column is wider: a way of suggesting that the children can be very active, that they have abilities other than the capacity to listen to a formal speech.
- The third column recalls the importance of 'timing'. With practice, we learn to have a good idea of the duration of the meeting.
- The fourth column incites one to vary the forms of interaction: each implies advantages and offers specific possibilities.

The dynamics of the development

What the file does not show directly is the movement and the rhythm of the initiative. This is important! After the welcome, the first activity must set the meeting on its course, gathering, awakening, motivating (1).

Then comes the properly so-called learning process (2): acquisition, appropriation. Finally, a phase of communication (3) allows the result to be consolidated.

Care must be taken, as much as possible, to make the two movements coincide: (a) that of the interest and the participation of the children with (b) that of the objective importance of the content. The peak of the children's participation should manifest itself at the most important (objectively) moment of the development. That is achieved by a good dosage of activities, of forms of interaction and means used: the most important and the most difficult should always be carried out in the most interesting way for the children.

Correlation

The itinerary of correlation (cf pp. 117-121) is often followed through the sequence and not in one sole meeting. This is the case in our example. At the time of a previous session, the children lived something (expressing oneself through an object) up to the level of the experience (what that does to me, what that tells me): stages A1 to A5 of the correlation methodology. In this session, they live stages B1 to B3. The stages C1 and C2, introduced here, will be taken into further account in a third meeting.

When prepared with care, your preparation files are a mine of gold!

Activity CATECHIST	Activity CHILDREN	mins.	Form of interaction	Materials/ Remarks
Recalls the last meeting. Directions for the 'Memory game'.	*'Memory game' Each child mentions the object chosen by someone else and recalls its meaning...*	7	*Circle*	
Launches the work on John. 'Jesus also found objects to express what he was... let us look for them.'	*From a first reference (6:35), the children look for all the times Jesus acknowledges and reveals himself in an object (cf p. 148: resources).*	10	*pairs*	*4 Bibles*
Directions for the decoding exercise. Discreetly follows and helps the children in their activity.	*Decoding exercise Each child chooses one of the texts. In his personal file, he visualizes what that tells him: (a) about Jesus; (b) about what he means to us, to me (all of John's 'objects' evoke a relationship).*	20	*Personal work*	*Personal files pens coloured crayons coloured paper scissors*
Animates the sharing session	*Sharing In an atmosphere of attentive listening and interiorization, each one can express what he has discovered (background music).*	10	*Circle*	*Tape for a tape- recorder*
Briefly adds the significance of the 'I am' (= God).		2	*As above*	

34. Evaluation

Each builder must choose with care how to build.
1 Cor 5:10

To evaluate is to examine, measure, discern in order to assess the value: what was well (or not so well) realized, what has value for the future (of the child or of the educator).

We often distinguish three kinds of evaluations:

1. *The summing-up evaluation* assesses the performances of the learner: has he achieved the objective? completely? partly?
   The educator can do it for himself. He can also do it with the child. This evaluation may be ratified by means of a more or less formal appreciation of the oral type ('Bravo, that's great!') or written (words or numbers: school marks).

2. *The formative evaluation* aims at awakening the awareness of the learner not only of his performances but also of his evolution, of his experience. A favourite form is the re-reading of it. In catechesis, it is certainly the most educative process.

3. *The prospective evaluation* aims at informing the educator about what he can or must improve in his behaviour, his way of speaking or doing. It consists in gathering, formally or informally, the opinions of the children about what they liked, what helped their progression, what blocked them. See below.

Appropriation

1. As a team, discuss the use of a summing-up evaluation in catechesis. How should it be done?
2. As a team, develop a few procedures for a prospective evaluation, for example:
   (a) a list of the spontaneous reactions of the children: these are useful to know how to observe and take into account (mimics, verbal expressions, behaviour) because they provide information about their interest and their participation;
   (b) a guide for interviews: during an interview, what questions to ask a child to obtain his opinion?
   (c) questionnaire-type to be filled in by the children.

For (b) and (c), do not forget to motivate the children warmly: 'I would like you to help me improve what I do, to make it still more interesting'; the areas to which it is useful for you to get their reactions: your behaviour, the activities you have proposed, the conditions of time and place.

The evaluation may lead you further: to supervision, to prayer.

Supervision

It is essentially a matter of re-reading the pedagogical activity

- effected with one or several other competent persons, for example: the one accompanying the leader of the session, the team of catechists;
- centred on the person of the educator (on what he becomes in what he is doing) and on the basic orientations of the educative activity (discernment of what is at stake, of tendencies, of possible reorientations, of difficulties). Here the technical aspects are of secondary importance.

Recommended!

The prayed re-reading

When it is re-read in the light of the gospel, my educative experience becomes the setting of my prayer. God gives me to see and hear something of himself. I set about to listen attentively...

This re-reading liberates profound energies, makes one discover the essential and renews the heart.

Recommended? Must we say so!...

Preparing oneself

The different evaluations will make us discover it: when everything has been prepared, there remains the preparation of oneself. Distant preparation: taking care of one's pace in life, respecting one's own person, finding one's stability as man, woman, Christian, since we educate first by what we are. Immediate preparation: taking one's breath, relaxing, going out for a walk, praying...

Evaluating in order to love

It is possible that at the beginning, the educator might be more preoccupied with evaluating and improving his procedure, his technique, his competence. That is normal: the children's respect is at stake. It is a matter of 'knowing and learning one's job'. Gradually, a truth will impose itself: to educate is to convert oneself; to change not only one's techniques but one's heart. Something easy – contrary to what we would imagine – because, there, God is the one doing the work...

Mt 11:28-30.

35. An active catechesis

Shout, sing, rejoice, dance, celebrate, play.
Ps 32:11; 33:1-3; 147:1

1. Why

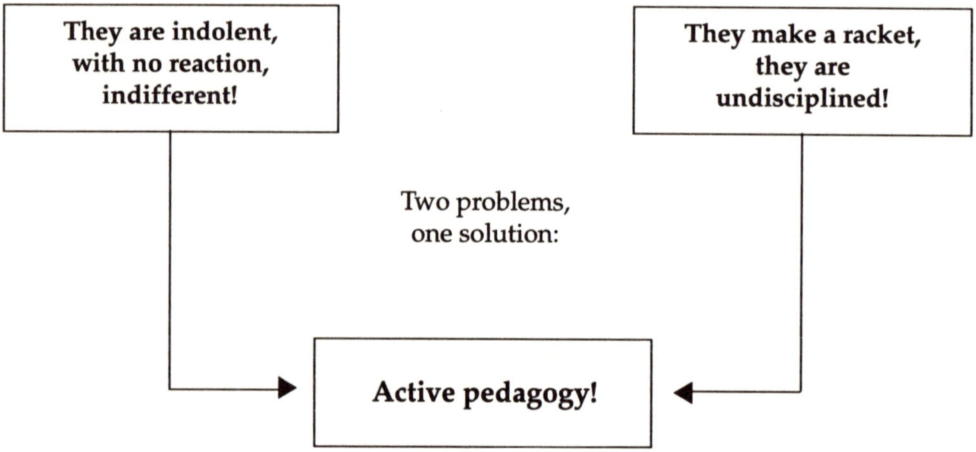

Children in good health, physically and morally, are a concentration of energy and creativity. Watch them when they play! Mobilizing and channelling that energy – there lies the secret of active pedagogy.

If you do everything (talking, explaining, demonstrating), they will do nothing or almost (apathy), unless they make a racket to liberate the excess of their vitality. They must, therefore, be stimulated and constantly provided with opportunities to be active in a constructive and educative way. But watch! activity does not mean activism nor agitation. If you overstimulate them or do so in an awkward way, they will lose heart (once again, apathy) or else, they will become overexcited (again, the racket). The whole thing is thus a matter of balance, and this chapter would like to help you find the correct one.

Appropriation

Before giving you a few indications, we beg you to find some yourselves by re-reading the chapters devoted to methodology (see children's activity, p. 141) and to correlation (pp. 117-121). From there, formulate a few good reasons to put an active pedagogy to work.

The reasons that justify an active pedagogy are not only human and technical, but also theological and evangelical. 'You shall love the Lord your God with all your heart, and with all your soul, and with all your mind, and with all your strength' (Mk 12:30): the child – like the adult – is called to respond with his whole being and with all his capacities. However, too often, we let him express himself with only a part of his possibilities. If we want faith to impregnate the whole life of the child, we must, within the catechetical initiative, take all his capacities into account: his memory and intelligence, to be sure, but also his affectivity and his aptitudes to play, move around and create. It is with all this that he is invited to give his response to God who is speaking to him 'in many and various ways', as the Letter to the Hebrews tells us (1:1).

This is of prime importance for our point: **activity and interiority do not oppose each other but are complementary, even interlocked**. Activity is not only exterior action but also what goes on in the heart. All true activity is at the same time a passion (to be touched, affected, moved, stirred). Similarly, every movement of the heart, every passion tends to exteriorize itself in action and behaviour. Action and contemplation are interior to each other.

Appropriation

Decipher the well-known diagram (above) in relation to our point. Share what it suggests to you.

2. How

> With this in mind, catechetical pedagogy, whatever method it follows, should stimulate the children's activity. If it fails in this, catechesis will not be able to perform its function of teaching the believer to give an increasingly personal response to the word and the gift of God. Such active pedagogy is not limited to external expressions, however useful, but endeavours to evoke a response from the heart and a taste for prayer. GCD 79

Let us straightaway dispel a possible misunderstanding. Active pedagogy is not synonymous with non-directing pedagogy, still less with a non-interference one. In order to stimulate the children to be active, to direct their activity to the objectives of the learning process, the educator will have to be active himself, to be very present to the children, to stay in control of the processes he has prepared, also to know how to accept and use the unpredictable.

At first, putting an active pedagogy to work comes up against certain elements of opposition which must be gradually overcome. The main ones are, most of the time, in the educator himself! The adult of today was often subjected, during his childhood, to a teaching in which the rules were: not to move, not to express oneself in a personal way, to keep silent and to perform tasks which were entirely programmed. Moreover, this teaching was addressed especially to reason and memory, leaving many other faculties undeveloped.

Children are perhaps your opportunity of going beyond your inhibitions! They are more spontaneous, freer, also more used to being active – the school has changed.

Appropriation

1. Make the inventory of the means of expression and communication you have experienced (training periods, sessions, formation, etc.) and with which you feel at ease.
2. Also make a short list of the means you have heard about without having experienced them yourself.
3. As a team, share your experience in this domain, not only by acquiring information for yourself but by informing each other.

Golden rules for an active pedagogy

1. **Observe the 'law of the 50%'s'**. By virtue of this 'law', half the time, at least, must be taken up by the children's activity.
2. **Hold back your knowledge to awaken that of the children**. Every time this is possible (and that is often), make the children search for the information rather than provide it yourself.
3. **Enhance the worth of the expressions** (verbal or not) **of the children, even when they are imperfect and hesitant**. You will thus make them confident in their capacity to express their faith. To enhance the worth does not mean to canonize, but to set off what is promising, initiated, fragile, still hesitant, in order to encourage the children to go further.
4. **Show your joy and approval in each progress**.
5. **Do not wait until you can express yourself brilliantly to stimulate the children to express themselves**. You are not a poet? Perhaps some children are. You do not know how to dance? The children will bring you along in their rounds... You do not have to be always the one showing them how to do things: they can find that out on their own.
6. **Vary the activities so that all the children can get something out of them**. This one is more gifted in a particular domain; this one, who writes with so much difficulty, will perhaps be an excellent mime actor.
7. **Work in the whole range of expression**: gesture, drawing, writing, speaking, singing, silence (why yes!...), modelling, cut-outs, games, etc.
8. **Put in a touch of humour in every meeting**. Children adore that and it has been proved that humour facilitates the learning process!
9. **If the children talk too loud, speak more softly**: you will obtain silence more surely and agreeably than by yelling.
10. **Do not humiliate**. Humour is not irony, still less derision or contempt. See rule 3.
11. **Do not make comparisons between the children**. They are all too tempted to do this themselves. Rather, encourage each one to be himself, herself: personal and different, happy about the difference in others.
12. **All through the meeting, be present to each, girl and boy**. Maintaining communication with each one in this way is the best method of obtaining discipline without having to impose it. You can be present by means of a word, a gesture, a glance...

Appropriation

Complete this list by adding your own golden rule.

3. From an active pedagogy to an active catechesis

What we have said so far could have been said of any pedagogical act. It was important to start from the general and fundamental facts about education. While granting full rights to these requirements, catechesis must, in some way, pursue them still further, by virtue of its own objective which is to foster an active faith.

This perspective is clearly emphasized in the Catechetical Directory.

Catechesis..., must evoke the act of believing (and also of hoping and loving); for accurate and firm judgement, the fruit of active education, here assist the acceptance of God's word... It is clear that active education is in complete harmony with the economy of revelation and salvation. The pedagogy which requires an active response from the recipients is in accord with the Christian life in general.

GCD 75

An active catechesis, therefore, is not simply a preventive remedy against inertia or the children's lack of discipline, but a condition bound to the very nature of catechesis. We can complete the diagram of page 150:

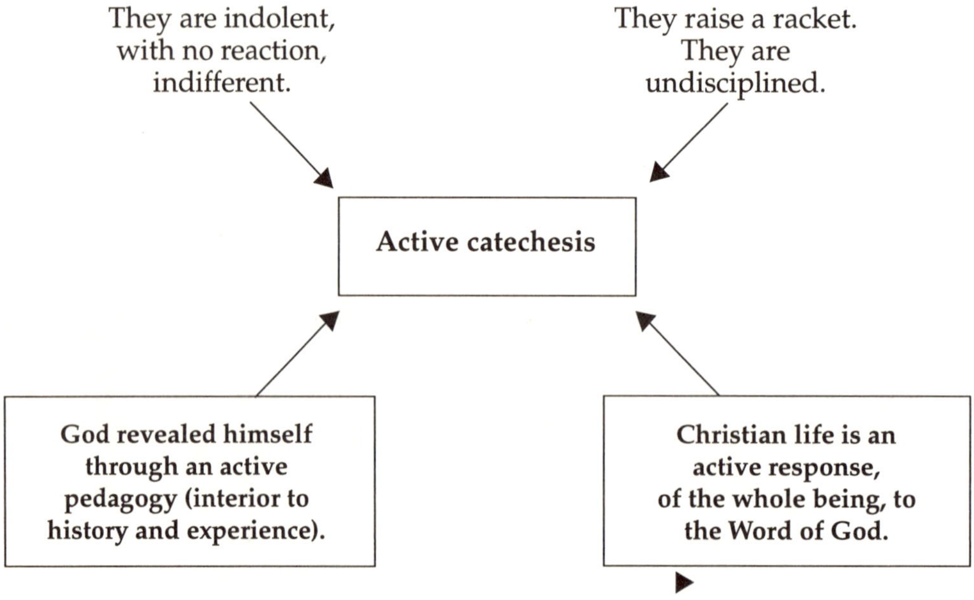

Appropriation

We sometimes hear the following objection: 'Revelation comes from God on high through the Bible and the doctrine of the Church, and not from us and our experience. Catechesis is the proclamation of this message and not a so-called pedagogy of experience.' In the light of this chapter, discuss this opinion.

Within the topic of activity, which is the topic of this chapter, we can show in a renewed way the structure of the catechetical act and indicate the specific axes of an active catechesis.

	Revelation	Catechesis	Faith response
AIM	Listening to the Word as a message addressed to me personally.	→ **WORD** →	Giving a free response to the Word by a personal and ecclesial profession of faith.
PEDAGOGICAL AXIS		↓ *Active correlation.*	
AIM	Interiorizing the Word so that it may touch my heart.	→ **MEMORY** →	Praying the Word of God and celebrating it with all my heart and my whole being.
PEDAGOGICAL AXIS		↓ *Education to silence, to interiority, to prayer and to celebration.*	
AIM	Accept the testimony of lives and experiences transformed by the Word.	→ **TESTIMONY** →	Make my life, in all its dimensions, the place for an experience transformed by the Word.
PEDAGOGICAL AXIS		↓ *Make the Christian experience (communion, charity) possible in the very interior of the catechetical act: relationships of quality, beginning with the pedagogical relationship.*	

Appropriation

A diagram can say more than a long commentary. For whoever takes time to read it. As a team, take the necessary time and share what the diagram tells you.

36. Motivation

Let anyone who is thirsty... Jn 7:37

To motivate is to whet the appetite. Motivating is an essential pedagogical activity, too often neglected. 'I was marked by the object of my thirst,' affirms E. Morin (*article quoted*. p. 85).

What makes us move

We have stressed this earlier, we really learn only what corresponds to a vital need. Review our list of needs (p. 68).

Against this backdrop, we can make out different forms under which these needs may manifest themselves.

Needs – motivations relative

- **to the results of the learning process**
  - DIRECT: acquire or increase a particular capacity or desirable faculty.
  - INDIRECT:
    - avoid a punishment
    - obtain a reward
    - please others
    - earn esteem or admiration.
- **to the difficulties of the learning process** — Overcoming a difficulty is stimulating. Watch for a good dosage! Too easy: not interesting. Too difficult: discouraging.
- **to activities leading to results** — The same goal, for example, knowing the Bible, may be achieved through various routes, more or less interesting to pursue.

In order to motivate, learn to play on these different keyboards:

1. Make an effort to stir the motivations that commit the child the most and which are most directly related to the objectives of catechesis.
2. Take into account the real children you are dealing with: what is motivating for some is not necessarily so for others.

How to get things moving

One could straightaway give a concise answer. The educator motivates:

- inasmuch as he himself is in motiμon, motivated and shows that he is so
- by proposing objectives (results) desirable for the children
- by setting up activities that are interesting for the children.

That being said, the catechist's mission can be made explicit in a more concrete way:

1. **He presents the objectives in an attractive and desirable way.**

   He awakens curiosity. In the film Heidi, the old teacher does not say: 'Attention, I have something very important to teach you.' He drops these enigmatic words: 'Children, if you only knew what I know!...' and all are eager to listen.

   He makes explicit the benefits the children will draw from the learning process. Rather than say, 'Today, we are going to talk about forgiveness', he declares: 'At the end of our meeting, each one of us will have found three weapons to use against meanness!'

2. **He fosters each one's growth of awareness of what motivates him and makes him move.**

   'Here, Yannick, you like to have a problem to solve... you, Juliette, you succeed much better when others encourage you... you Carol, you love the stories from the Bible...'

3. **He endeavours to make the motivations evolve and he tries to clarify them.**

   He will lead the children to have the experience and to become aware of what is most profitable and desirable for them, that is, in the end, that we live not only from bread but from the Word of life. From elementary needs, the children will move to deeper needs (without neglecting the first!).

   He will help each one to personalize his motivations. 'Benedict, pleasing others, being a success in the eyes of your friends, all that is fine, but the most important is what matters to you, deep down in your heart.'

   From 'human' motivations he will trace a path toward motivations of faith and charity. That is done less by speech than by the progressive and intimate experience of a faith and a love which, in themselves, are a power of joy and freedom.

Appropriation

Take any session of catechesis (from your practice, from a textbook) and, with the help of the guidelines of this chapter, bring out in the open all the interplay of the motivations concerned or that you could bring into play. Identify those which, to you, appear to be the most educative.

37. Language and catechesis

You have not spoken of me what is right, as my servant Job has. Job 42:7

... now Job had no difficulty in inveighing against God and in expressing his anger and his doubts to him, whereas his pious friends outdid each other in repeating the good theology of the times. And Job is the one, says God, who spoke well! Before attempting to see through this, two stories...

•

This takes place in a restaurant. A customer, a stranger, called the waiter and ordered:

– Single, a coffin, please!

Surprise... up to the moment when the client pulled out a dictionary from his pocket and proved that, in French, waiter is sometimes synonymous with single, and coffin is a bier!

Words do not always have the meaning we think they have...

•

The king's son had gone mad and thought he was a turkey. He spent his time, naked, under the table, gobbling like a turkey. All the educators and all the physicians were summoned. In vain. Until the day a holy rabbi happened to pass by. He took off his clothes, went down on all fours and joined the prince under the table. And there, he gobbled with him. On that day, a new life began. Some time later, the king's son was behaving and speaking like you and me.

Sometimes, we must go down on all fours to give the word...

•

The 'problem' of language in catechesis could be represented by this diagram:

Variable geometry
The mission of catechesis is to increase the dark shaded area. That is done by increasing zones 1 and 2. Zone 3 increases by the very fact, provided we do not put up any obstacles.

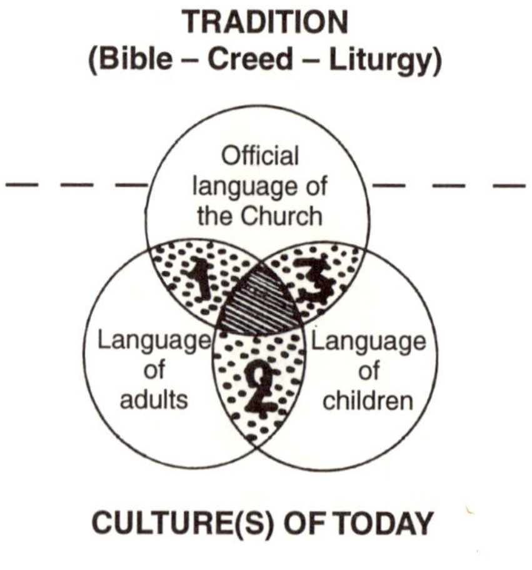

There are many languages used to express God and to speak to him. The Bible is the best proof of that. Praise, shouts, stories, visions, letters, judicial codes, poems: everything speaks of God. And what a variety of confessions of faith: Peter's solemn declaration (Mt 16:16), questions asked by some (Jn 6:42), tender gestures of love of the sinful woman (Lk 7:37-38)...

The proper function of catechesis is to establish permanent links among the three types of languages: the one in which the Church recognizes and expresses herself with authority; the one of the adults, the catechist; the one of the children, considered collectively and individually. The dark shaded zone of the diagram indicates the overlapping sections of these languages: these sections are the areas of catechesis.

Note that all these languages themselves are bathed in the surrounding cultures which change with time and geographical regions.

A few orientations:

1. Be aware, catechist, that your language is not the whole language of the Church. Stay in the 'overlapping zone' (**1** on the diagram) and try to extend it. It is from there that your word is both yours and that of the Church.
2. Construct a language common to that of the children (**2**) and, for that, begin by listening to them and learn their language.
3. Do not forget that the children also have to discover the zone of their language 'overlapping' that of the Church (**3**). You cannot do this for them but you can help them by giving them the Word and the right to speak, in multiple languages (verbal and non-verbal).
4. The privileged overlapping (dark) zone is the celebration in which the community, adults and children, allow themselves to be reached by the language of God's word and gestures, and respond to him in faith, with words and gestures.
5. The 'area of truth' of all languages, is the heart of the believers: the 'area of verification' is their lives.

Appropriation

1. In this perspective, re-read the chapters devoted to the 'language and rites' of a group (pp. 90-99) as well as the one about correlation.
2. Analyze the interplay of languages in the text of B. Ritter, quoted on page 111. Note particularly the role attributed to the Church.
3. Also, in the perspective of the language, review the chapter 'For an active catechesis'.
4. Draw a few practical guidelines from the three stories quoted on the preceding page (Job and the two anecdotes).

1. The language of relationship

We shall briefly deal with three types of language. The first one concerns the relationship between the children and the adult. The tragedy of certain catecheses is that this language is almost totally neglected for the benefit of the sole language of instruction. However, the language of relationship comes first: it speaks more loudly than the language of instruction which, without it, remains dead.

By language of relationship, we mean here not the relationship at the level of feelings and intentions, but the relationship inasmuch as it is expressed and spoken with words, moments of silence, behaviours.

The content of catechesis, remember, is not only a certain knowledge about God but the encounter of the Word with our experience. However, a whole aspect of this content, of this experience, is not part of the programme. It emerges. It turns up as the meetings take place, including (possibly especially) in the unexpected.

The evaluation, the re-reading and the supervision owe it to themselves to take this aspect into account as a priority. Before asking myself, 'How did I speak to them about God and about faith?', I will ask myself, 'How did I speak to them the language of God and the gospel in the depths of our meetings and our relationship? Did I hear their questions? Did I understand their profound, existential requests?'

In the Gospels, we certainly see Jesus making use of the language of instruction, but we are especially struck by his manner of expressing God without necessarily naming him, through a language of relationship which makes the other exist in his humanity and in his dignity as a child of God. 'Come… have no fear… you are not far from the Kingdom... I do not condemn you...' For Jesus, the two languages (relationship and instruction) express the same thing. What about us?...

On our diagram, the language of relationship is zone 2, in the dotted part, that is, not yet 'baptised' by the explicit words of the faith. The diagram clearly shows that if this zone does not exist, neither can the central (dark shaded) zone.

Appropriation

1. Did you ever hear someone give you a 'word which makes one exist as humanity and in the dignity of a child of God'? Remember... was it always and necessarily while speaking of God? or otherwise? how?
2. Did you ever give such words to 'your' children? Remember... As you think this over, do you see 'missed opportunities', questions which you pushed aside because, at the time, they appeared to you to be 'disturbing' or 'not on the subject'?
3. Relationship is not expressed only with words, even if these have a decisive impact. Remember as well a particular relationship important to you, which was being lived, or is still being lived, especially in gestures, behaviours.

There is the catechesis you have planned, and what we could call the 'parallel catechesis', the one you do, possibly unknowingly, in your language of relationship. In order that the two converge and come together, here is a tool of reflection and evaluation.

A plan for 'parallel catechesis'

1. Messages exchanged before and after the properly so-called session (note the expressions of the children, your responses...)

2. Unexpected, strange, 'disturbing' questions or reactions during the session (expressions of the children, your reactions):

(In this wide margin, make notes on your re-reading, what you 'hear' perhaps better as distance in time grows... the questions you are asking yourself... the things to follow up or to be launched again... the link with the 'official subject' of the session...)

Appropriation

Use this plan, as an exercise, to re-read a meeting or again the itinerary of the last month.

2. The language of instruction

Catechesis, to a large extent, also relies on the language of instruction: presenting, informing, making others understand.

Putting this active pedagogy to work does not reject this language but integrates it in a more complete initiative.

- In order to speak well, the catechist will learn from the great masters. He will take the time and the means to reinforce and broaden his 'zone 1' (see diagram, p. 162). Habitual reading of the Bible, of the great and good Christian authors (some were or are remarkable catechists). As he draws from these sources, he will enrich his own language of faith, as much in depth as in soundness and precision.
- That being said, allow us to insist a little on another complementary point.

'Language is the home of the being, man has his dwelling there', said a philosopher (Heidegger). That is very true: we indwell our language, it is our home. But there are many places in the immense house of language which differ according to persons, generations or groups.

Words are rarely limited to the one meaning found in the dictionary. The meaning of a word is also its 'affective load', what it evokes for me in relation to my history and my experience.

When we teach, we use words which echo within us. Do they have the same resonance in the mind of the children? Nothing is more doubtful. In spite of all our precautions and our explanations, we do not have a direct hold on the meaning of words for the child. God, Father, love, sin, forgiveness, trust, heaven, salvation: when we say these words, the child perhaps hears something altogether different from what the catechist means.

The only way of avoiding misunderstandings, serious distortions, even unwholesome misinterpretations, is to allow the child to speak. Letting him react and reaching him in his own language. Accepting, from the innermost depths of our 'zone 1', that the child builds his own 'zone 3', little by little, by feeling his way.

When he is reached in his way of understanding and expressing himself, the child, in turn, will be able to make his way into the language of the Church, to grasp its real sense and communicate the truth in this way.

Let us not forget that, on the other hand, in spite of all the explanations, the words of faith yield their secret progressively, as the spiritual experience is developed. A journey of the whole life and not the simple acquisition of notions, once and for all.

Appropriation

Choose a strong word from the religious language (God, Father, etc.) and see how this word has probably taken on new meanings, perhaps quite different, for you, throughout your whole existence. At a particular moment of your childhood, of your adolescence, of your life as an adult. Put these different meanings and their sequence in words. 'At a particular age, the word God, for me, evoked... today, it evokes...'

We were given the bite with Jesus

An institution for maladjusted children and young people. Hurt by life, they have often had dramatic experiences. Abused, surely.

On that day, I had planned to 'talk to them a little about Jesus'. Jesus, this word transgressed their outer space like a terrible UFO. A red alert! and their AAD triggered off the shooting.

- Nothing to... from Jesus!
- I don't believe in him.
- He is a ...
- First, he never existed. Pastors are the ones who...

I sum up. They took a good twenty minutes to execute the 'enemy'. Stunned in the middle of this crossfire of the machine guns, I was asking myself interiorly; 'Why?!...' All the more so that in their voice and tones, there was a violence revealing the extent to which they felt attacked.

The following week – in the meantime, I had pondered - I made a vague allusion to this episode and I told them the classical story of the two types of men and the word 'dog'. The first had been cruelly bitten when he was small: the word 'dog' frightened him. The other had been saved by an avalanche dog: whenever he heard the word 'dog', he was radiant with joy.

I did not need to explain. I was still in the process of telling the story when Joâl literally jumped on his chair, eyes shining:

- This is exactly like us! we have been bitten by Jesus. And he evoked this Jesus who commands this, prohibits that, brandishes fear and threat. Abused...

My catechesis? To live with them the whole phase of breaking down this distorted language, sometimes perverse, about God or in the name of God. Letting them cry, explode, while interiorly blessing God (exteriorly, doing what I could!): this rejection of a 'lousy God' (excuse the expression), is this not already a burst of faith, the cry of a yearning for the true God?

By my presence, I express God, my capacity to reach them, to love them. Someday, perhaps, a new language about God will spring forth, the fruit of an encounter between their faith and mine.

Appropriation

1. From the religious point of view, no child is a blank page when he comes in catechesis. His head and heart are full of ideas on God, on sin, on life and death. Good ones and distorted ones. Have you ever been confronted with these images?... Recall the one or the other experience...
2. As a team, discuss the following opinion: 'Teaching is, first, cleaning out the mind of what pollutes it... only then, can we sow.'
3. What appears educative to you in the above message?

3. The language of dialogue

At the precise meeting point of the language of relationship and the language of instruction, there is the dialogue. An exchange in which each partner speaks – his own word – and gives this word as a gift, not as a stroke of the fist. Each is also accepting to receive the word of the other as a gift, and not as a threat.

From the true exchange, there emerges a new truth, a new language which says more and in a better way what each partner already knew.

To us, the dialogue, the exchange of words, appears to be an essential element of catechesis. Nothing takes its place: neither the audiovisual techniques nor the most sophisticated didactic methods. It is powerful and effective because it establishes relationships among persons. In catechesis, the dialogue is, so to speak, the translation or the parable of a more profound reality: the mysterious exchange of words between God and the child.

We sometimes deplore the number of hours children spend in front of the television. 'Some have more hours of television in a week than hours of catechesis in a year!' Perhaps. But let us not forget too hastily that one hour of true dialogue will have a greater impact than thousands of hours spent in front of the television.

We all live from words that were given to us in a true exchange. And in certain stubborn silences, we waste away. Dialogue makes us live. Again, it has to be a dialogue...

... for there exist imitations, counterfeits, secondary products. Pedagogy or teaching are not exempt from them. Didactic questioning (sometimes useful, often deceitful) which pretends to question to 'make others find' the right answer; questions of sheer form of which the reply is known to everyone; programmed 'dialogues' in which the teacher is thrown off if he does not obtain the answer (so evident), that he had foreseen on his file or in his head...

Dialoguing can be learned.

There are several excellent methods and good studies on dialogue and communication (cf the Gordon Method, for example). The essential can be summed up in a few 'rules':

- listening attentively
- rewording the other's message (explicit and implicit) to make sure we understand each other.
- speaking in 'I' (rather than in 'we' or 'it must...', etc.)
- warmly inviting the children to exteriorize themselves, to express their opinion or their feeling; giving them frequent opportunities to do so.
- never forcing one to speak, not 'worming secrets out of him'.

Appropriation

With the children's consent, tape ten minutes of dialogue during an upcoming session of catechesis. A dialogue of which you are the animator. After a start-up phase, the children are not intimidated by the microphone. Listen to it at your home. Better yet, transcribe the text and analyze your performance, alone or as a team.

Samples: what do you think of them?

- *When you come home from school and you tell something to your mother, what does she do?*
- She prepares the meal...
- As for me, she is not there, I open the door with the key...
- *So you, Dennis, your mother is preparing the meal, but as she is cooking, what does she do when you tell her about what went on in school?*
- She, too, watches the clock...
- *Yes, she looks at the time because Daddy will soon be home, and what else does she do?*
- ...?
- *She listens to you?*
- Yes, she listens to me.
- *You see, she listens to you. When we love someone, we listen to him or her. Who else still listens to us?*
- Daddy, he listens to me.
- Me, my brother...
- Daddy does not always listen to me.
- *Ah yes!... but there is Someone who always listens to us!...*

•

Stephen — Zacchaeus wanted to see Jesus... there were lots of people, so he could not see.

Teresa — Yes, but he wanted to look at him. That was because he was interested in him, so he climbed up a tree.

Catechist — *What happened then?*

Stephen — Well, Jesus saw him and said to him, 'Come down from your tree, Zacchaeus, I am going to your place.'

Catechist — *And you, Yves, you were saying that Zacchaeus changed after meeting Jesus. Have you any idea about that?*
... silence...

Peter — Because Jesus trusted him. Often, I think that... Zacchaeus was a sinner...

Stephen — We don't know if he was really a sinner... perhaps the others were the ones who...

Peter — The others, they were there to say bad things about him... but Jesus placed his trust in him.

Catechist — *Yes, I understand what you mean...*

Susan — As soon as Zacchaeus saw Jesus, something changed in his heart.

Catechist — *You believe that this happened when he saw Jesus?*

Peter — Yes, when he told him, 'I am coming to your house.' He said to himself, 'There, he trusts me.'

Appropriation

Here is a list of behaviours which may facilitate the dialogue: allowing to speak, challenging, making one express his opinion more precisely, asking a good question, referring a question to the group, clarifying points of agreement and of difference, rewording (the words, the ideas, what we think we understood in the words), bringing divergent information, stimulating exchange among the children, refocusing the discussion, not interrupting the silence... Complete, qualify and, as a team, make this list more explicit.

38. The symbolic experience

And the Word became flesh... we have seen his glory.
Jn 1:14

1. Man, a symbolic being

In the previous chapter, we dealt with verbal language, the word. We will now consider another type of language, every bit as important: symbolic language.

The word 'symbol' comes from a Greek term meaning: putting together, joining. Originally, this word designated an object used as a sign of recognition between partners. Two friends, for instance, would break a fragment of glass at the moment of a prolonged separation. Each would bring half. Years later, they or their children could recognize each other by bringing the two pieces together. If they fit perfectly, they testified to the covenant and the given word. The pieces acted as proofs (for example, cf Tb 5:1-3).

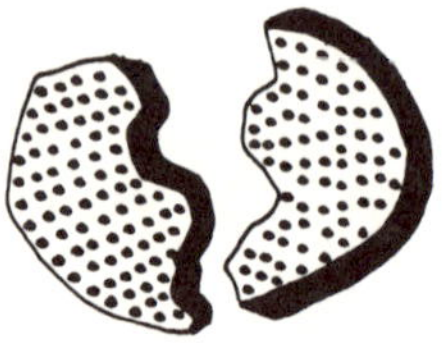

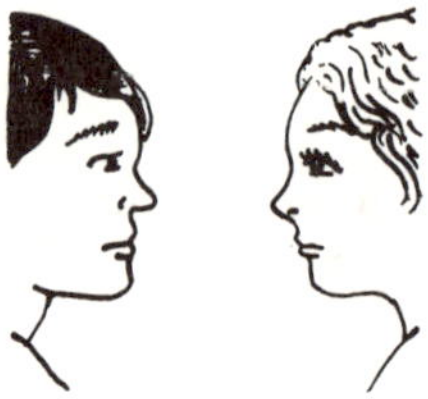

Therefore, a symbol is:
- a material reality (the divided fragment)
- which expresses and communicates a spiritual and invisible reality (friendship, trust).

The symbol, par excellence, is the body of the living man. In him, the visible and the invisible have a rendezvous. A material reality, the body is at the same time the place and the witness of a spiritual venture: knowing and loving. Every event that involves the body also involves the spirit. Everything that the spirit experiences takes place in and through the body. Our body is the flesh of our spirit. It brings our spirit into the world of history.

Man is a symbolic being, that is, he is a citizen of two worlds, the visible and the invisible. The symbolic and nonverbal language is all that allows these two worlds to come together, to be spiritually present to itself and to others in a way different from that of the word: language of the body, gestures, objects.

Appropriation

Revelation sheds a new light on all this. We invite you to discover it yourself through a short biblical journey. Gen 2:7; Jn 1:14; Jn 20:22; 2 Cor 4:6-7, 16, 18: read these texts; see, in your Bible, the notes and references in the margin. Also re-read pp. 104, 105 and 107 of the chapter on correlation. To conclude, make a short synthesis on the theme: 'Man, a living symbol in which the visible has a rendezvous with the invisible...'

Living is a symbolic process

1. Human experience is structured symbolically. In other words: every corporeal reality (the visible) is the opportunity and the means of a spiritual (invisible) realization of man.
2. It is through this symbolic process that man has a rendezvous with himself, with others and with God. This is how he fulfils himself as 'a being capable of knowing and loving'.
3. The key moments of this process are:
   - an event that 'touches my body'; I perceive, I do something, I feel in my body;
   - a word that seeks or explains 'what that does to me or what that tells me';
   - an awareness: I discover better who I am, who I can be, who I want to be;
   - a covenant (inaugurated, renewed, renounced) with myself, with others.
4. The setting of this process is the world (nature, the objects with which I came into contact). Everything can become a symbol. Certain elements are privileged settings: the body itself; the body of others; the earth, water, air and fire.

Awareness and speech

The two are strongly linked. We place speech before awareness for the sake of simplicity: this is how things happen at the most apparent level. But awareness, in reality, implies several levels or several moments. Before speaking, even before reflecting explicitly and clearly, we have a first intuition, more or less conscious: 'I don't know how to tell you this, but it affects me!... somewhere, it speaks to me...' The word allows the awareness to become clearer, sharper, more precise. It also allows one to identify the links between various experiences and draw guidelines for life. The word expresses what, already, was there, sensed in a confused way. It broadens it, links it and makes a project of it.

Appropriation

After reading these pages, we propose a few ways for you to experience what we have attempted to evoke:

1. Go for a swim or take a shower, or again light up and watch a fire, or stretch out on a secluded spot in the meadow, in the forest. Experience this with the greatest awareness possible: your sensations, what that does to you, what that says to you...
2. Choose, in nature, a small gift for someone (it could be for yourself). Look, touch, smell, ask yourself what that does to you, what that tells you...
3. When you return home, re-read this chapter!

2. Pedagogy and symbolic initiative

We have seen that the human and spiritual experience could be built and transmitted:

– by the active contact with mediations (see chapter on correlation)
– by the word (previous chapter).

The symbolic experience, centred on the living body, is a third language used to communicate at the level of experience. Third in our enumeration. In fact, it is the first, the most elementary one. We experience things before we express them. We constantly exchange non-verbal messages with our environment: nature, objects, persons. We are more or less conscious of that, but 'somewhere, that does something to us, that tells us something'.

Taking a walk all by yourself in the forest, touching somebody's face, gazing at the stars: so many symbolic experiences where the visible in us reaches the invisible. Our communication with ourselves and with the world is like a three-storey pyramid. At the bottom, the large base of our silent and symbolic contacts (that affects us... that tells us...). Then the middle storey: what we say about it in words. Finally, the narrow summit: what we objectify in mediations like letters, intimate journals, tapes, photos, works of art or crafts.

Oddly enough, traditional pedagogy did practically the opposite: many contacts with documents (mediations), quite an abundance of words, few non-verbal symbolic experiences.

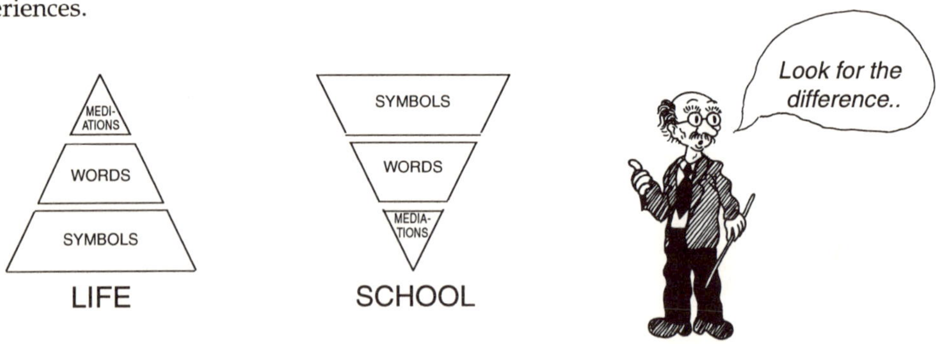

Today, we are rediscovering all the possibilities offered by the language of symbolic experience. With certain children (when verbal expression is blocked or deficient), it is even the favourite language. In catechesis, the symbolic initiative is especially indicated: because of the Word made flesh, because the body is temple of the Spirit, because of the sacramental perspective (the life of God through the mediation of others, of gestures and objects).

Appropriation

You probably know a certain number of non-verbal games or activities which could be integrated into a symbolic initiative. Make an inventory of them and share it with your team.

3. The symbolic initiative in catechesis

Gathering together, getting in touch, looking at each other, shaking hands: all these are symbolic experiences. The presence and the relation, there is no end to the fact that it does and says 'something somewhere'.

Against this backdrop, precise initiatives may be put to work. They are summarized in the following sequence:

LIVING AN EXPERIENCE ▶ SPEAKING OF IT ▶ SO THAT I MAY BECOME AWARE OF WHAT I AM, (for myself, for others, for God).

Whereas the traditional pedagogy was satisfied with 'speaking about' the experience, here the experience is first given to be lived. Let us make the three phases of the symbolic sequence more explicit:

1. **Getting in TOUCH**: with space (taking one's place, moving about...)
   with things (that we touch, that we handle, that we make...)
   with one's body (posture, breathing...)
   with another's body (looking, dancing, shaking hands...)
2. **SPEAKING**: What did that do, say, to me (to you, to us)? (at the affective level and emotions, sense level)
3. **AWARENESS**: appropriation, interiorization, rewording or celebration.

After a symbolic experience, the word is generally more personal and freer. Awareness has a better chance of being effected (we do not remain at the level of an intellectual understanding).

For example: a catechesis on faith, trust placed in God and the Church. It could begin by the 'game of the blind': each one, blindfolded, allows himself to be led by someone else for ten minutes. After a verbalization of this experience (what that did/said to me?), the children will undoubtedly be in a better position to understand what walking in faith, like the disciples, like Abraham, really means.

> In the subsequent chapters, you will find other suggestions concerning different elements which may be part of a symbolic initiative (body, singing, etc.).

4. Power and risk of the symbolic experience

The symbolic experience has a character of power and universality. Power, because instead of designating an experience with more or less abstract words, with more or less 'neutralized' expressions, it connects directly with the experience, it grasps one's guts, as we say. Universally, because, at one go, it sets in motion everything that can move in you: your senses, your nerves, your imagination, your memory, your feelings, your thought.

We draw your attention to a few phenomena inherent in the symbolic experience:

1. It awakens the inner world of the imagination and phantasms. If everything goes well, this world enters into a dialogue with the objective reality and the symbol springs forth from this confrontation between a more or less controlled imagination and a reality. But the imagination can also fall into panic and 'devour' reality. For example, watching a beautiful fire in the night can allow you to dream and become aware of the 'fire' within yourself. But if you are like the pyromaniac fireman, fire can play on your desire for power, your unconscious yearning to become 'the master of fire, the devourer who feeds on what he burns'.

2. It exercises a strong emotional impact. It will probably touch each one in his area of sensitivity, fragility, vulnerability. If all goes well, this promotes life and healing. But it happens that anxieties are awakened, that old and 'forgotten' wounds are touched to the quick. Reactions in a group will probably differ according to the persons. That is fortunate: they can mutually counteract each other. It is also a risk: the emotion of one person can become contagious and a source of trouble for the others.

3. It bears abundant and multifarious meanings. A symbol, a symbolic experience never has only one predetermined meaning. Water, fire, earth may be signs of life as well as of death. In the abundance of possible meanings, each will seek his own path. It is true that certain symbols are more or less coded and that we can, therefore, count on a probable significance:

- because it is linked to elementary experiences of a universal character, for example, the sun, symbol of life, night, symbol of death;
- because it is privileged by the cultural environment, for example, the child, symbol of innocence and purity. But let us not forget that within a culture, there are also mini-cultures proper to each group and that, besides, the code may be modified.

4. It brings processes of identification into play in which the imagination plays an important role (individual and collective imagination). The educator can channel this phenomenon by providing himself with the framework for the identification, with a story, staging a scene. For example, an experience with water may be set up as a situation while telling an episode of *The Little Prince* (the well) or a story of bedouins in search of an oasis, or John 4 (cf p. 191).

Rules of the game

From the above, one may draw a few practical guidelines:

1. In order to know how far is 'too far' in the symbolic experience, a good knowledge of your group is indispensable. And a good knowledge of yourself.

2. Prepare only symbolic experiences or activities that you yourself have lived (the team of catechists may be a laboratory of trials).

3. Instigate discreetly a true session of verbal self-expression while respecting the freedom and the personality of each. Do not manipulate but exploit the abundant richness of meaning by rewording, by reinforcing, by establishing links, by making the common points and the differences obvious.

4. Set aside some time and means for awareness (interiorization and communication/celebration).

5. Your symbolic initiative is, of course, an initiative of correlation. Therefore, carefully identify the possible points of connection between experience and revelation. Besides, this preliminary reflection will allow you to anticipate a situation which will somewhat channel the imagination and the emotions. Thus, in the example mentioned earlier (the game of the blind), you can dispel in advance certain anxieties by straightaway establishing a context of trust (by means of a story or a short recollection).

6. Re-reading is indispensable in order to know how each one has lived the experience.

Appropriation

As a team, think of a symbolic experience lived by someone among you. Do a re-reading of it in order to discover: (a) the different phases evoked, p. 169; (b) the extent to which the phenomena quoted p. 170 have played a role; (c) the extent to which the 'rules of the game' have been respected.

39. The body and the gestures

David danced before the Lord with all his might.
2 Sam 6:14

> With the language of his humanity, God comes to find the hands, the face and the bodies he directs to himself and who respond to his own.
>
> Michel de Certeau,
> *La Faiblesse de croire,*
> p. 22, Seuil 1987.

> The gesture is what commits one; it is never pure thought nor interior emotion (...), the gesture precedes, underpins, supplements and prolongs the word. There is a language of gestures which, for being less differentiated than articulated language, is more radical. Before the words, springs the gesture. And there where the words stop, the gesture goes on – were it but in a silent presence.
>
> J.-B. Molin, in
> *Dans vos assemblées,*
> J. Gélineau ed., vol. 1, Desclée 1971.

In this chapter, we shall attempt to evoke the language of the body by using powerful quotations and drawings. Some methodological indications will help you, here and there, to transform what the texts and the pictures may have helped you understand into pedagogy.

These pages, of course, are as valid for a symbolic approach, like the one just described, as for prayer or celebration.

Appropriation

1. In a to and fro movement floating between the texts and the pictures, let yourselves be imbued. Be aware of what that does and says to you.
2. Practise the suggested attitudes.

Seated

to listen
or to share
Lk 10:39; 2:46;
Mt 5:1

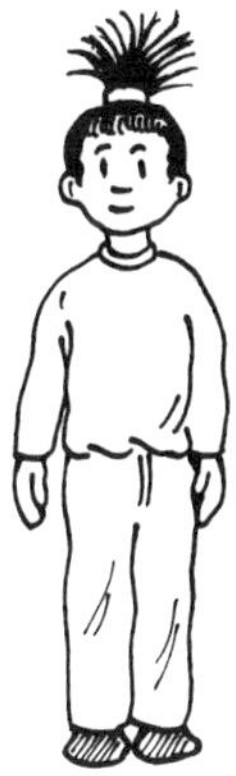

Standing

like a tree,
the one walking,
the risen one
Ps 1:3; Jer 17:8;
Ex 12:11; Ezek 2:1;
Acts 7:56

Kneeling

or on one's knees
to ask,
to worship,
to fall down
Acts 9:40; Lk 5:8;
Lk 22:41; Mk 14:35;
Gen 17:3

Gestures 'to speak to or about oneself'

striking one's breast
(Lk 18:13)
making the sign of the cross
hand on the heart
hands opened out
head in one's hands...

The humble offering of the body is already a total gift: 'This is my body', preceding, like the prow of a ship, the impulsive enthusiasm of the heart and being followed by well-ordered thoughts that never measure up to the gesture, (...) A murmuring of the heart in the silence of the body.

Not being magical, the gesture needs the word to make of it a call or a recollection.

The gesture is acceptance and response at the same time as desire and anticipation. It already grasps now what it must yet seek.

Man in prayer, 'this tree of gestures'.

(These quotations are taken from M. de Certeau, op. cit., pp. 13-19.)

For a pedagogy of the gesture

1. Learn to 'dwell' in your body (sessions, exercises).
2. Plan some time for preparation (relaxation, concentration).
3. Learn the correct posture (spinal cord, neck, nervous and muscular tension: relaxed without slumping).
4. Breathing is an essential element for all postures and gestures (learn to breathe from 'way down' as in sleep, become aware of the breath...).
5. Help to give meaning (suggest words, interior attitudes corresponding with the corporeal attitude... few words, but powerful ones...).
6. Help to develop awareness (during and/or after) of what that does and says.

Appropriation

In an attitude in which you feel comfortable, allow your breathing to become the symbol of the most profound movement of your being: breathe in (I receive, I receive myself), breathe out (I give, I give myself). The two mutually call each other. If I cease to 'give' or to 'receive', I die stifled...

Walking
like Abraham,
Jacob,
people in an exodus,
the disciples...

Gestures of the hands
to express peace,
the covenant,
forgiveness,
poverty...

Removing one's sandals
like Moses at
the burning bush

Closing one's eyes
in order to see within
and from within

40. Space and things

Surely the Lord is in this place and I did not know it!
Gen 28:16

Man is at one with the world and space. He is in a perpetual and silent dialogue with his natural and material environment. Forms, colours, distances, consistences, waves move about. Man is influenced and marked by them. But, in turn, he puts his stamp on the universe, he projects himself in it and expresses himself there. Space is our largest body. And in space there are objects. There is Someone.

1. Making one's dwelling

A place to live, a house: shelter, intimacy, space for communication. With doors and windows to go in and out. Inside, an atmosphere. Rather, atmospheres according to the 'areas': kitchen, living room, my bedroom, the space around my bed.

Children are very sensitive to 'the soul of places'. In order to feel at home, welcomed, they need to explore, to organize, to mark out their territory. There is an age for cabins or tents, for secret nooks in the garden or in the forest.

Let them dwell in the catechesis room. Organize it a little, put in their colours. Along with them, create an ambience: tidiness and beauty, cleanliness, but also, occasionally, noise and upheaval. Organize your space, even if it is limited. A 'prayer area' will be respected and recall the benevolent gratuitousness of a given space, which is of no use but where the stranglehold of the functional is loosened.

Introduce them, physically and spiritually, into the space of a church. Prepare this visit (learning how to behave, walking slowly, living in an attentive silence). Initiate them in little doses: entrance and exit rites (genuflection or bowing, sign of the cross), walking about, sitting, standing, the altar, the stained-glass windows, the baptismal font, the place of forgiveness...

2. On the move

No dwelling is definitive. To live is also to pass on, to leave, to go 'to the land that I will show you' (Gen 12:1). 'A wandering Aramean was my ancestor' (Deut 26:5) and so are we.

Prayer or catechesis on the move means pilgrimage. Going into exile, taking risks, walking for the sake of faith, in response to the call of the inner Word which sets the whole being in motion. Itineraries of catechesis can project themselves in space: large or small pilgrimages (perhaps there is a shrine in your area), ways of the cross, meditative walks, liturgical processions. The 'rules of the game' are the same as for gestures: making a proper movement (we can learn to do that), breathing, providing meaning, becoming aware.

There is also dancing and all the rhythmic and choreographic activities: rounds, farandoles, etc. A way of expressing oneself, of communicating, of being part of a shared joy.

Finally, movement may be proposed as language and pedagogical means. To play or celebrate the parable of the prodigal son, we can, for example, designate within the space (of a hall, a church, a yard, a glade) the different 'areas' of the parable: the house of the father at the beginning, the garbage place, with the pigs, etc. Each can go where his heart summons him and experience something. Then to move about according to the inner initiation.

Appropriation

1. Meditate on the various areas of your dwelling. Go to a precise location. Explore with your senses (sight, touch, smell...). Think of what you are experiencing there, what this place does and says to you. Make this your prayer.
2. Do the same in a church.
3. Do the same on your way from your home to the church, from the church to your home.
4. Do the same in nature.

3. The objects we find and which find us

In the symbolic order of things, objects are more than objects. Every object can take on a meaning and speak to our heart as to our intelligence. Each thing and each aspect of that thing (colours, etc.) fulfils several functions for us:

- function of a SIGNAL for our biological survival (it makes us do something: escape, eat, spit out again, etc.)
- function of RELATIONSHIP to set us within the human network of communication and exchange (that does something to us, emotionally)
- function of MEANING to enrich or modify our system of representations (that tells us something)
- function of ORIENTATION (the resultant of the three others) to confirm, to make the project of our life more explicit or to change it (that makes us be someone).

The symbolic value of an object is linked to these four functions, with a particular emphasis on the second and the third. In catechesis, the symbolic objects have many uses:

1. They can be objects of **projection or identification**. We have given an example of this in the chapter on methodology (pp. 144 and 147). We can use them as a 'photo language' always available. For example: 'Look for an object which, for you today, says something about friendship...' Materialized metaphors.
2. They may become **language of prayer and celebration**. Let us listen again to Michel de Certeau:

'Of all the objects that it, like a tree, holds in the network of its gestures, prayer makes its dialogue with God. The body symbolizes with things. (...) If, like gestures, one of the objects is prayer, these represent the sequence and the stages of it under the form of relationships within the world which tacitly reveals God. Kissing the cross, picking up the book or (...) hands busy telling the circular rosary, the pray-er not only prays in the midst of things, but with them; nature, of which his body is a part, provides him with something to speak about to the Father of things, visible and invisible...' (op. cit., p. 21).

4. The things we make and which make us

To make is to take part in the act of creation. According to our potential, the making or transformation of objects makes us partners of the One of whom we are the image. Making something is to bring into existence what did not exist before. It is projecting into matter a little or much of myself. In the object thus created, I can recognize myself. Born of me, when it is before me, it tells me who I am. It can say it to others, too, and become a language piece.

Drawing, painting, modelling, assembling, sculpting, giving form or colour (including to one's face: make-up, masks; or to one's body: clothing, finery): all these activities have their place in an active catechesis. They can intervene at different moments and for different purposes:

- in the initial stage, enter into a theme, raise interest, motivate, allow a first projection of what the children carry within themselves in regard to this theme;
- in the stage of decoding a document: retranslating it into another language is often a good way of understanding it (for example, translating from the written form into a painting, or vice versa);
- in the interiorization stage: providing some preparation and a favourable climate, the modelling or the drawing may be meditation (while we are doing it and after, in contemplation);
- in the communication and expression stage (even in celebration): the fabricated objects then become mediations through which the experiences are shared and transmitted.

Appropriation

1. On a large piece of paper, write: 'To conclude, the children make a small drawing to illustrate the lesson.' With a thick felt pen, make a cross over this sentence meaning that you are ruling it out from your catechetical vocabulary. On the remaining part of the sheet of paper, note the 'thousand and one' ways of doing some other thing and in another way.
2. On this page or on the previous one, underline two sentences which help you to understand what Jesus did on Holy Thursday ('... he took bread...'). Between what Jesus did and what we do, what similarity, what difference is there?

41. Time and catechesis

He has made everything suitable for the time.
Eccl 3:11

The human body is a mixture of space and time. The body has its rhythms and its durations. It keeps a memory of the past: it is imbued with memories it lives in the present time.

1. Time for catechesis

Acceleration of time, whirlwind of schedules, stress: the children themselves are caught up in the spiral of time going crazy. Cut off from natural rhythms, our time splinters away into a thousand activities and constraints.

Finding time for catechesis, outside of school hours, in addition to the training sessions of football, guitar lessons, music practices, homework, is sometimes the problem. We, the catechists, can contribute to its solution by doing the impossible, and even a little more, so that this time be most profitable. A good moment of the week, anticipated and desired by the children.

The limited amount of time at our disposal can urge us to go for quality, to go to the essential. This means careful preparation. Basically, the less time we have with the children, the more time we must devote for them (in the preparation, in our own formation), so that the time spent with them is full and rich with the time that we will already have sacrificed (made sacred) for them. And during the session, we will truly be with them, devoted to them, for them. We will give them some presence.

There are several ways of managing the time of catechesis with the children. A good formula appears to us to be the combination of weekly sessions (about one hour) and some 'intense moments' (semestrial half-days, annual weekends, for example). The weekly hour may seem to be a small thing. It is true that, hardly begun, it is already the end and that in so little time we can hardly get great activities going. But it has the immense advantage of repetition and of a rhythm which allows continuity.

Appropriation

Meditate on your agenda. How much time do you devote for the children without them (preparation, formation, re-reading, prayer)? What do you think of this? Do you see anything to change, for your good and for that of the children? Discuss this as a team.

2. The catechesis of the time

Time, with space, is the most fundamental cultural mediation (cf p. 109). Before the invention of writing, the organization of time and space was the principal way of expressing, objectifying and transmitting the system of representations and significations proper to a culture. The space was organized symbolically: heaven and earth, a spiritual geography of the places on high, sacred precincts, etc. Time also, with its rhythms and feasts, linked to those of nature (seasons) and to man's labour.

In spite of the increased number of cultural mediations (writing, printing, transmission of images, etc.), space and time remain the two great parameters structuring our experience. We have just recalled the importance of space, of places and objects. The catechesis of time also is decisive: it adopts the symbolic perspective of the liturgical cycle.

This cycle is structured along three axes:

- the weekly period culminating in the Sunday celebration;
- the annual period, a true invisible Bible, which, each year, makes it possible to celebrate all the aspects of the Christian mystery, all the great events of salvation;
- the vital period which is the itinerary of a life marked by the sacraments, those of the great moments (baptism, confirmation, matrimony, holy orders, anointing of the sick) and those of the route (the Eucharist and forgiveness).

Catechesis, itself, is structured along the sacramental axis (the third above) since it accompanies the Christian initiation of the children. It can also make an important contribution to the experience of the other two periods, the liturgical week and year. We shall limit ourselves to pointing out two facets of this contribution:

1. The pedagogy of the symbolic elements of liturgy. Initiating the children to the language of signs, objects, colours, gestures proper to each liturgical event. Helping the children to see them, to understand them, to live them. There lies a whole richness that catechesis can bring to the fore.
2. The challenge to the Christian communities is that:
   (a) the liturgical celebrations be done particularly carefully, be beautiful, lively, prayerful, making use of every possibility (often underused) of the liturgical resources.
   (b) the children and the young people be truly welcomed and able to take their place. Otherwise, how will they have the experience of the Christian community gathered together?

Appropriation

As a team, with those responsible for the community, examine your own actual situation on these two points mentioned above. Set yourselves some objectives for the near future and decide how you will achieve them.

42. Singing, music and silence

Miriam... and all the women went out after her with tambourines and with dancing. And Miriam sang to them: 'Sing to the Lord.' Ex 15:20-21

Song and music speak to the heart and mind, create a climate, a communion where the 'current' runs through and brings forth a silence of plenitude from which they themselves have sprung.

1. Singing

Singing is a symbolic experience of many facets:

- it expresses (and awakens) emotions, feelings, not filtered or cooled by concepts and abstractions
- it is gratuitousness and breaks through the framework of the functional
- it forms community: by ATTENTIVE LISTENING which gathers in the same setting of attention and emotion; by the ACT OF SINGING, especially: adjusting oneself, harmonizing in the difference of voices
- it is a sign of celebration.

According to G. Stefani, in *Dans vos assemblées*

How to learn a song or hymn?

- have the children listen to it (cassette or record)
- read and savour the text (structure, key words, movement)
- become aware of the rhythm and practise it if it is somewhat difficult ('singing' the song on one note only... la la la... da di da...)
- learn the melody by making them savour it with its nuances, phrase by phrase.

Composing a song on a known melody

A good means of communication and collective creativity.

Pedagogical reminder

The singing must be integrated into the pedagogical initiative, like an element which elicits progress (and not as a 'stop-gap'). Multiple uses: appropriation, expression, celebration...

Appropriation

According to whether you are spontaneously more sensitive to the aspects of the text or the music of the song, practise listening to the other aspect, the one you favour less, by examining a song of your catechesis.

2. Music

In broad terms, music fulfils the same functions as singing, with a particular accent on the dimensions of the gratuitousness and the emotion, in the absence of words making the meaning explicit.

Its principal uses in catechesis are the following:

1. As a cultural mediation, some music (or some singing) may be heard and decoded (what it does to me, what it tells me) in order to enter into communication with the spiritual experience which has brought it forth: religious music or with a religious dimension, hymns in a foreign language (we are not 'captivated' by the words): Greek Orthodox singing, Gregorian chants, negro spirituals...
2. Music can accompany and 'adorn' an action: procession, swaying, dance, march, corporeal expression...
3. It can also lead to interiorization (by its soothing effect, its capacity to induce a peaceful nervous tension): in this case, choose music which is rather 'loud' to produce a beneficial effect on the nerves, but discreet enough to be forgotten.
4. It is also possible to make some music: guitar, recorder, xylophone, percussion instruments...

3. Silence

Idonotknowifyouhavealreadythoughtaboutthis,
butsilenceistothewordandtothenotesofmusic
exactlywhattheblanksandthespacesaretotheletters
andthewordsofasentence.Similarly,themargin
hereontheleftistheplaceofmeditationtowhichthe
textrefersyoutoprolongyourdrea

In catechesis, silence is indispensable in two types of activities:

- those which claim **the attention to something or to someone**: contemplating, listening, committing oneself...
- those which consist in **interiorizing, in becoming aware, in paying attention to oneself, in praying.**

Pedagogical art does not consist in having no need of claiming or imposing silence (just the same, there are exceptions!), but in creating the conditions which induce the silence of attention and of interiorization (exercises of preparation, of relaxation, of attention; the way of presenting a mediation: tone, intonation, delivery, mimic and the posture of the educator).

Appropriation

Imagine three ways of leading the children to silence without having recourse to injunctions or constraints.

43. Pedagogy of the image

He is the image of the invisible God. Col 1:15

It has often been said that the Word invites to live and sets in motion, whereas the image convenes to the repose of contemplation. A gaze of faith which, in nature, sees the work of God and his invisible perfection (Rom 1:20), a gaze of faith which, in man, recognizes the divine resemblance (Gen 1:27) 'to give it back to God' (Lk 20:24-25), through Christ, perfect image of man and of God (Col 1:15; 2 Cor 3:18) in whom we are transfigured.

There are also images or pictures, the works of our hands. Here are a few ways of using them in catechesis.

1. Reading the image

Because of television, children are used to the merry-go-round of images, not necessarily to the contemplation of one image. Through the aggressive publicity of posters and magazines, they are used to being shocked by images, not necessarily used to reading them in an active and educative way. Civilization of the image in our times? Not so sure, possibly much less so than in the Middle Ages. Our relation to the image is restless, violent, often superficial, when it is not perverted by an excess of sensations or by an unbridled imagination.

However, there is a treasury of images or pictures, paintings, photos, reproductions of art – which are true cultural mediations, powerful means of conjuring and transmitting experiences.

It is important that children be put in contact with such images. Through them, they will be able to construct and organize their interior world, as much the one of their imagination, with all its emotional charge, as the one of their knowledge. But such an approach supposes a true learning process, an initiation of which we present, we think, a few key moments:

- a phase of relaxation and the creation of an atmosphere (movements, music, breathing...)
- putting in the presence, by no means trivial, of the image: a few words ('we shall look at a masterpiece... thousands of people go to see it in the museum...') or a small staging (changing the setting, putting out the light for a moment...)
- a first naïve contemplation
- expression:
  - (a) what do I see (forms, colours, traits, details, structure, etc.)
  - (b) what does that do to me? what do I feel? (emotions, feelings...)
  - (c) what does that tell me? (the artist has wanted to say that... it is the story of... this is to say that... it makes me think of...).

Rather than using cheap 'sentimental' pictures, draw upon the wealth of art and iconography. Powerful images (this does not mean sensational images).

2. Slide projections or audiovisual montage

This is often more a comic strip than pictures to contemplate.

Certain montages lend themselves to a use similar to that of reading a picture. If there is a sound track, the language of the music and of the words will be taken into account. It is often useful to have two or several viewings, interrupted by short dialogues, for example:

- First 'naïve' viewing
- dialogue: each is invited to mention one picture which has struck him, one word which has meant something to him;
- Second viewing (it is enriched by what the dialogue has clarified)
- instructions for work, personal or in a group, in view of an appropriation or of taking a stand, etc.

3. Photo language

This well-known technique, with its numerous variations, lends itself to various uses: presenting oneself, introducing a theme, building a problematic or a synthesis.

It is most interesting, for it is a powerful means of triggering off personal words and it fosters the creation of a climate of interiorization and attentive listening.

4. Children's drawing or painting

We have already said that this should not be the only activity proposed to the children. On the other hand, when used judiciously and when it is connected to the pedagogical initiative as a whole, drawing remains an attractive and educative means, as much for expression as for interiorization.

It is also an excellent support of communication between the child and the educator, among the children. This supposes a period of dialogue and listening: **what the child says about his drawing is almost always more important than the drawing itself.**

Appropriation

1. In this book, you will find different types of pictures: illustrations (mirror-like, opposite the text), diagrams, graphics, pictures to be looked at for their own sake. Identify them and evaluate their pedagogical function.
2. It is also useful to set up for yourself a small treasury of pictures, photos and slides, classified according to theme.

44. Games

We played the flute for you and you did not dance.
Lk 7:32

Catechism is serious. But for the children, so is play. Conclusion: catechism and play should get on happily together... since both are serious.

1. Playing for the sake of playing

Watch the children play. Get into their play if they invite you. In this way, you will truly be with them, in their world, and new possibilities of relationship will be offered to you. Seize the opportunities when they present themselves. Instigate them at 'intense moments' of time, half-days, weekends, when the programme is lighter.

2. Getting-acquainted games

Or of renewed knowledge. They are many. They have the advantage of freeing the word, of allowing a different communication, often richer because removed from stereo-types and inhibitions. Two examples will be enough to whet your appetite for them.

Ball or network. The children are sitting or standing in a circle. You throw the ball to a child: he can then say something to make himself known (name, what he likes, favourite game, birthplace, etc.). Then he passes it on to another and so on.

Variation: if the 'ball' is a ball of yarn, its movements back and forth weave a net, the symbol of a network, of a group with its bonds.

The marketplace. We are at the marketplace.

First period: people come and go, unknown to each other; they wander in every direction, indifferent, observant, curious or uneasy, the ones with respect to the others (that can be done with music, a kind of fun fair).

Second period: at the same marketplace, we know quite a number of people, the number of encounters grows, we greet each other, 'good morning', 'good evening', we talk about the weather, we indulge in small talk.

Third period: same situation, but this time we meet friends we have not seen for years; the joy of seeing each other again, the wish to talk about ourselves and to listen to each other (every time the music stops, we change friends).

N.B. An evaluation, even brief, is useful: what I liked, liked not so much; what that did and said to me. This comment is valid for all the games.

3. Interaction and communication games

They allow us to take our place in the group and in relationships in general. They also offer possibilities of communicating in other ways.

The 'game of the blind' (p. 169) was an example of this.

In this category come also the role-playing games: about a theme, a situation or an opinion, some typical characters are assigned and set on a stage. They are given to voluntary players who are given a few minutes to prepare themselves, after which they spontaneously play their roles, by getting 'in the shoes of the character'. A period of discussion allows each to explore what each one has felt or observed.

Other games favour a more open communication or a better cooperation in the group.

4. Simulation games

These games offer the possibility of living complex situations 'on a small scale', such as economic relations between rich and poor countries (the banana game, for example). They are better suited to the older children and require relatively long periods.

Appropriation

We have only been able to make your mouth water. Draw up the inventory of resources available to you in order to know more about this: specialized studies, experienced persons whom you could ask for a few tips... that you would adapt to suit your style, not without having tested them yourself...

45. Narrating

Then they told what had happened on the road.
Lk 24:35

Children adore stories. They could listen to some of them hundreds of times. Adults, besides, are constantly telling stories: what happened to them, what happened to So-and-so, what went on at work, etc. Not to speak of films and novels which tell so well stories of life, of love, of suffering and of hope.

Why is it so important, so interesting to tell or to listen to stories? The first two paragraphs will attempt to answer this question. The next four will be more practical.

1. Life is a story
Only humans have a story

Humans alone have a story. Plants, animals and stars have none: they are only an unfolding, more or less programmed, of physical, chemical, biological facts. A chain of events with no consciousness, no memory, no project. In other words, with no experience (cf p. 106).

As a conscious and unfulfilled being, a being of desire, man has a story. His life is a story in the making, reaching out toward a fulfilment of which he himself is the free actor. Develop the awareness of the difference between life as the unfolding of a chain of biological events on the one hand, and this same life viewed as the story of your personal becoming linked to the collective becoming of men.

Your biological development, engraved in your cells, is, on the whole, the same as that of all the other members of the human race, and you cannot do much to change that. Altogether different is your story, the one you are living within this chain of biological facts. It is unique. No one has lived this story before you and neither will anyone after you. Thousands of people have lived similar events, no one has experienced them the way you do. It so happened that you were born, had a family, went to school, worked, married, like so many others. That is not your story. You have lived these events in a particular way, you have had a particular experience of them, you have interpreted them in a particular manner: that is your story.

Besides, when we give an account of something that happened to us, it is not a simple relation of facts that we give, but what it does and says to us. That shows up even in the choice of words, the intonation of our voice, our mannerisms. We are involved in what happens to us.

Appropriation

Spend half an hour alone and tell yourself your own story, through a few experiences you judge to be the most significant ones. A support may sustain your attention (writing, drawing).

2. From fairy tales to the glowing impulse of the wish

Scholars have studied tales, these imaginary stories which are one of the riches of all cultures. They have tried to discover the structure, to explain how they function and their psychological impact. By basing ourselves more specifically on the research of some of them – V. Propp, A Greimas, B. Bettelheim – we propose that you make a little detour through these tales.

They all start because there is a LACK of something: someone is unhappy, confronted with a difficulty which puts his life or his happiness in jeopardy: for example, Cinderella is abused, humiliated. At the end of the story, the wish either comes true ('they married, were happy and had many children'), or is launched again in a positive and dynamic direction.

Up against a thousand and one obstacles and enemies (witch, stepmother, wolf), but relying on a thousand and one resources (a good fairy, a magic object), a HERO will conquer and obtain what was lacking. He has to overcome some ordeals:

- An ordeal that qualifies him as a hero capable of conquering what is lacking: he must prove who and what he is. In the story of the quest for the Holy Grail, for example, it is a matter of pulling out the sword from its magic rugged sheath. The hero alone will manage to do this.
- A decisive ordeal by which the hero will win the victory over that main enemy. The knight kills the dragon.
- A final ordeal by which the hero is acknowledged as such, is crowned with the glory of a hero and receives his reward: the prince marries the princess.

These tales, basically, tell our own story, not in what is unique about it, but in its profound and universal movement:

Man is a being of desire. For him, living is to project himself into the infinite dimension of his desire. By going through the trial of what is lacking for him, at the level of being (identity) and love (relationship), he is called to fulfil himself totally, according to the impulse of this desire which is at work in him and uplifts him as an invincible promise.

At the level of the imagination, tales tell us the dynamism of this story and promise us its success.

What we call sacred history tells us, at the level of the reality seen from within – the reality of the reality! – that our desire is the mysterious echo of a Word which is calling us and keeps its promises by being more faithful to us than we are to ourselves.

To tell a story is to offer a model of interpretation and orientation of life.

Appropriation

1. Re-read your story (exercise of the previous page) as a sacred story, that of your desire inhabited by the Word of God. Rediscover the great moments of your developments of awareness in faith, of your personal conversions: when you consciously said yes to Jesus Christ.
2. Imagine a tale. Tell it.

3. God revealed himself in a story: tell this story

If it is true that to know God is to know that he loves us and to love him in return, then God could not make himself known in any way other than by living a story with us. Otherwise, we would have known only one idea of God, but not God himself. We truly know someone only by sharing his story.

Each of our personal stories interlocks in some way with other stories forming with them a collective story which, ultimately, is the story of all of humankind. In Jesus Christ, prepared by Israel and continued in the Church, God connects the whole human history and, therefore, each of our individual stories, on his own, the story of the gift of his love.

Telling a story, a tale, for example, is a way of interlocking the mind, the subconsciousness of the child in a movement which leads him to live his story as a trial with a 'happy ending'. It is nourishment for the imagination.

Telling the story of God with men, the Bible, is to offer the child a connection with the most secret and the truest movement of History. It is to give him the assurance that his story will also succeed, will end well, not because of a dream but because of a promise which has already met with its full realization in the risen Jesus. It is nourishment for the imaginationand for faith.

An essential task of catechesis is to tell the story of salvation, the events of that story, the 'wonders that the Lord performed for us'. A catechesis that does not tell stories loses its vital link with Revelation and transforms itself into theory, into ideology.

We take the liberty of insisting on this for three principal reasons:

1. In our rationalizing culture, we are tempted to treat the explanation of ideas and concepts and the argumentation which sustains them as a priority, even an exclusivity. The explanation is necessary, but it holds a second place with respect to the account.
2. The power of the accounts is to relate the events as such, without reducing them to ideas. A faith called to be event itself is born and nourished with accounts of the faith. Argumentation produces rather intellectual certitudes: these convictions, while not being alien to faith, fall short of faith.
3. Stories help us to construct our own life while respecting our freedom. They propose without imposing.

Tell the story of the Bible, tell that of Jesus, of the Church. Explain when and as you can, but, Great God, do not stop telling this story.

Appropriation

1. As a team, look for the respective advantages of various ways of telling the Bible: oral account, account supported by fabricated characters or by puppets, mimed account (which can lead to a home slide projection).
2. Point out the objections sometimes made to biblical accounts: 'There is violence and bloodshed!' 'Miracles nourish a magical faith.' Discuss these opinions.

4 . Re-reading: the story of salvation in the process of being made!

Time and again (references in the margin), we have had the occasion of emphasizing the importance of re-reading and of suggesting to you how to do this. We will be satisfied here with reminding you of that. The story of your catechetical group, the story of each child – and your own – also need to be told as experiences of salvation, as sacred stories. That is done by the process of re-reading. Through that, you will progressively discern, and the children as well, how God manifests himself and allows himself to be encountered in the humility of your journeys. You will discover the truth of this song: 'Every man is a sacred story.'

5. Biographical accounts

Lives of saints, lives of Christians of today, famous or not, direct testimonies (invitation, interview of a character, inquiry based on documents, slide montages, video cassettes): there are accounts on which we can connect our imagination while waiting to connect our experience onto the experience of which they are witnesses.

6. Wisdom accounts

We find some in every culture and every religion. As tales go, they are fictitious but they speak the truth at the level of experience. Some have no lack of depth nor of kinship with the gospel.

Examples: *The Little Prince* (Saint-Exupéry), the story of the beggar asked by the prince about what he has to give him (R. Tagore). But, all the same, this is not the gospel... The Old Testament also contains marvellous tales of wisdom, which have no lack of scope: for example, the books of Tobit, of Jonas, of Job.

Appropriation

Do yourself a good turn by telling a story to yourself: make the characters of the above comic strip speak.

7. Stories, means of indirect communication

The 'secret incentive' for stories is that they commit one to a process of identification.

The reader, the listener or the spectator of a story projects some aspects (real or imaginary) of his own personality onto one or several of its characters; he recognizes himself in these characters. He identifies with them, at least momentarily and partly.

Thanks to this process of identification, the stories become good means of discreet, indirect communication.

Characters summon or are rejected – consciously or not, it matters little! – they create a volume of expression for the personality.

Besides, as we can hide ourselves in the characters of a story we are telling, we can provide others with the opportunity of discovering themselves there again!

Thus, the child can reveal what he is and let himself be reached without baring himself and being confronted too directly with himself.

An educative communication founded on the identification with the characters of a story, can take on various forms:

- dialogue with the child on the story and what takes place in it: 'Why does So-and-so do this?... What does he want?... What does he feel?', etc.
- free re-translation of a story by the children (mime, puppets, etc.).

The educative value of this type of communication is linked:

- to the psychological and spiritual finesse of the educator;
- to his discretion and respect for the personality of the child;
- to his respect for the temporary and limited character of all identification: the purpose is not that the child become this or that, that he be like this or that person, but that through his different attempts at identification, he may find and build himself up.

Formal examples are found in the Bible (2 Sam 12:1-7), particularly in some of Jesus' parables (Lk 7:41-43; 10:30-37; 15): these stories are a communication that connects directly with the experience of the listeners.

Appropriation

1. Try this out yourself with a text from the Gospels. With whom do you identify yourself? Get into the story by putting yourself in the shoes of this character: what is going on? what do you feel? what do you want? what are you doing?
2. After hearing the account of the Prodigal Son or of the Good Samaritan, the listeners of the past and those of today may realize that this is about themselves.

8. The tightrope walker above an abyss

Note on the tragic aspect of life

Popular tales are not bed-of-roses stories. In the midst of fairies, witches and dragons, the hero goes through terrible ordeals which are the stage-setting of our anguishes and our wish to come out of them victorious.

The Bible, from cover to cover, is a story 'written in blood', the kind that makes the heart beat, that cries out to God, the kind given out of love. Light and darkness, suffering and glory, misery and tender love appear on every page. Why?

Living is a drama in which happiness and misery are engaged in a struggle of which man is both the battlefield and the stakes. And the essential seems to escape his hold. What he is, his own mystery, his destiny, the terrible matter of his death: because he is conscious, man sees this abyss of *why*, but he is unable to clarify it completely. A tightrope walker above an unfathomable void, he goes through life, now dancing, now on the tightrope of fleeing time.

In the interweaving of the needs that can satisfy him, man is obsessed by a mad desire, that of knowing and loving infinitely. But this unlimited power of the desire is at the same time the source of an extreme vulnerability. I cannot conquer this love I am thirsting for by force, I can only hope for it, ask for it and receive it. What is most necessary to me is at the same time what does not depend on me, but on the free gift from another person.

Happiness and misery are thus bound to this interplay of freedoms which give or refuse themselves. But at the heart of his freedom, man experiences evil. Not only misfortune or mistake, but evil: the wound consciously and freely inflicted upon oneself or others. Not only the mistake but the sin, inasmuch as he discovers that, in his limited existence, there is the interplay of an absolute, the 'yes' agreed to or not to the Love which alone can give a fulfilling existence.

The child is plunged, from his first day, into the half-light of this strange existence. He, too and sometimes painfully, experiences something tragic and the process of learning to walk, of stumbling like a tightrope walker above the abyss.

The powerful stories of the Bible reach him at the heart of this experience. They tell him the Word that allows him to journey in trust because there is Someone. In the tragedy of the history of men, God came down to make the power of resurrection spring forth. Let us not make a light story of this.

Let us not blot out from the Bible whatever deals with the vital questions and the drama of life. Let us not either turn a deaf ear to the cries, more or less stifled, that the child will possibly attempt to articulate by evoking his difficulties in life, his doubts, his pain. If we do not know how to answer, let us offer a loving silence. Finally, without being complacent about this, let us not omit from our catechesis the reality of the shadows of life, of the failures, of suffering and sin. In order to allow all this to enter into correlation with the mystery of Easter (cf p. 171).

46. Memorizing

The word is very near to you; it is in your mouth and in your heart. Deut 30:14

Memory is an extraordinary faculty. Thanks to it, we can provide for ourselves an interior library which is always available. Moreover, contrary to ordinary libraries, this one is active: the information we have stored enters into our mental circuits and interacts with other information. Far from being an inert stock, what we know by heart enlightens and guides us even if we are not always aware of this.

To know by heart is also to belong to a community of language and meaning, to acknowledge oneself not only as one of its members but a subject capable of accepting and giving the received Word.

Like these safe paths, beaten by thousands of marching feet, particular formulas of prayer or of faith can be engraved in memory and trace out an itinerary of life.

Making children memorize good things judiciously is to allow them to build an intellectual and spiritual treasury for themselves.

Here is a list of good things to memorize:

- the Our Father
- the Creed
- the Beatitudes
- the Ten Commandments
- the Rejoice, O Mary
- texts of the Gospels (the 'recitatives' with gestures from the rhythmo-catechesis may be useful)
- prayers and hymns of the Mass
- beautiful morning and evening prayers
- psalms
- songs and hymns
- short and concise doctrinal formulas hinged to the synthesis of the Creed.

Appropriation

1. Complete or modify the above list in regard to the actual children that you are accompanying. Check your choices with other catechists.
2. Try to recite for yourself three sentences from one of the Gospels. Then check how exact and faithful your performance is.

47. Praying

Lord, teach us to pray. Lk 11:1

Watching Jesus pray awakened the desire to learn to pray like him in the hearts of the disciples. It is by watching his educators pray (first his parents, then the priest and catechist) that the child will be stirred to pray.

Education to prayer is at the heart of religious education. Prayer, indeed, is the inner space for the intimate encounter between God and man. Between God and the child. To neglect this aspect would amount to reducing religious education to a cultural veneer or to a conditioning of exterior behaviours.

At the same time, prayer is the sacred place for the greatest freedom and the greatest secret. As educators, we will always be limited to preparing it, fostering it, giving it a good means of expression and a structure – which is a great deal without, however, having a direct hold on it. Discretion and respect are, therefore, imperative, but they do not mean giving up or being indifferent.

1. A four-point programme

Education to prayer implies four 'moments'; these are linked together without replacing one another: passing to the next 'stage' must not rule out the previous stage but prolong it.

1. PRAYING	Before being an educative task, prayer is a grace and, we might say, a right to Christian life. Before being an educator, I am a believer and, therefore, prayer is at the heart of my spiritual life.
2. PRAYING BEFORE THE CHILD	I can witness to this life of prayer in front of the child. Inasmuch as I have an affective relationship with him, he will be in contact, synchronized with my attitude of prayer: by seeing me, by 'feeling' me in prayer. That is particularly true in early childhood, when the child is entirely nestled in his parents' affection.
3. PRAYING WITH THE CHILD	Gradually, the child will spontaneously enter into the exercise of prayer, not only by exterior imitation but by a need to 'pray his desire and his life'. The educator will help him by being present at the mumbling of his prayer.
4. TEACHING HIM TO PRAY	While respecting the journey of the child, the educator will try to sustain and guide the movement of prayer in the direction of an increasingly Christian prayer, of an increasingly pure and free prayer, of an increasingly evangelical prayer.

2. Accompanying an evolution

Since it is an intimate relationship with God, prayer is closely linked with the image of God to which the one praying is referred, consciously or not. To educate to prayer and to reveal the true face of God are thus two facets of the same activity.

The spiritual evolution of the child is interior to his psychological growth. Without wanting to mark out the stages very precisely, we can nevertheless describe the major aspects of this evolution.

1. **From a prayer in symbiosis to a personal prayer**

The child begins by immersing himself in the prayer of his parents. Somewhat like the disciples in that of Jesus. But it would be hardly educative to transform that prayer into dependence. On the contrary, the child will be encouraged to find his own movement and his own expressions. (Because they have not followed this route, some adults keep on praying only when they are dependent on a guru, an ambience.)

2. **From a manipulative, utilitarian prayer to a gratuitous prayer**

The child can pray to God because he expects something from him, because he imagines him to be almighty and he would want to use this power to his own advantage. Or because he is afraid, he feels God as a threat, the cause of the misfortunes happening to him: could these be punishments sent by God? Educators will take care not to fix the child in such attitudes, something which could happen if they manipulate the prayer of the child, if they make it an occasion to blackmail him ('Ask God to forgive you and promise him you will not start again, otherwise, he will know how to catch you at the next turn of the road!...').

3. **From an anthropomorphic prayer to a prayer turned to God**

'Anthropomorphic' means 'that it resembles man'. A vision of God is such if it attributes to him our feelings, our qualities and our shortcomings. At first, the child imagines God as a super-adult. In the image of his father, God is surely authority and power par excellence. In the image of his mother, God is absolute protection and security. Educators will help the child by taking opportunities to say that God is Other. He is not the one resembling us. We are the ones made in his image and who reflect this resemblance very imperfectly.

4. **From an animist prayer to a Christian prayer**

'Animist' means that the child attributes a 'soul' to things and events. Beyond the happiness and the misfortune happening to him, he 'sees' a mysterious presence having beneficial or evil forces. Let us not entertain animism by giving it a Church sanction. Let us rather educate the child not to see God 'behind' everything that happens, as if he were pulling the strings of events, but rather as the One who is a Presence of love in our hearts, in happiness as in misery, when we are 'nice' and when we are 'mean'.

5. **From a ritualistic prayer to a free and true prayer**

Rites give a sense of security. There is an age – late childhood, preadolescence – when observation of rites responds to an almost magical logic. In order to free themselves from a more or less diffuse feeling of anguish, children constrain themselves to precise, almost obsessional observances. Prayer and 'religious practice' can be caught up in this circle. While favouring a sane ritualization (regularity, security of gestures and formulas), educators will bring to light and value the attitude of the heart and the quality of the intention.

6. **From a prayer centred on self to a prayer centred on God**

Prayer centred on self is an 'improved variation' of the utilitarian prayer. Surely, it no longer asks for rewards or material favours but sets for itself the goal of personal development and moral growth. Such a prayer must not be objected to – no more than the prayer of petition centred on 'favours' like health, happiness, etc. – but it needs to be directed in order not to imprison the one who prays within the limited circle of his biological or psychological needs. The impulse of the desire has another impact since it projects us toward the infinity of God. Christian prayer leads us progressively to pray by looking not from ourselves to ourselves, but from ourselves to God, and even from God to ourselves. It does not seek to entrust God with the projects (even good ones) of our will, but to accept the project of his will which surpasses, in excellence and favour, everything we can imagine.

(We have drawn our inspiration here from
A. Godin, *Le Dieu des parents et le Dieu des enfants*, ch. 3.)

To accompany also means not to press on. When we want too much 'perfection' too quickly, we risk blocking rather than helping. To accompany is to take small steps along with.

Patience and respect are the main requirements here. Children do not all pray in the same way. Children do not all have the same rhythm of spiritual growth or the same spiritual sensitivity. Educator, remember your own evolution: perhaps you do not pray today as you did ten years ago. Nor like a particular friend you know...

Appropriation

With the help of the guidelines of this paragraph, take stock of your own life of prayer. Where are you at? What lines of evolution constitute a call for you?

3. Christian prayer

We have already outlined its characteristics in the previous paragraph. We can now recall its specific structure:

With and through Christ, the Christian says 'Father', in the Spirit

1. **With and through Christ**

   'Through Christ, our Lord': this is the conclusion to the prayers of the Mass. Prayer turns us to Christ our Saviour: Have mercy on me, a sinner! Face to face with him to identify ourselves with him. This reference to Christ manifests itself:

   1. by a privileged contact with the gospel, meditated and prayed;
   2. by participation in the Eucharist, source and summit of the Christian life.

2. **Father!**

   With and through Christ, we turn to the Father, the origin and mysterious term of our desire. To say Father is to receive ourselves from him, is to let him make us exist through the gift of a love that surpasses our expectation. It may therefore astonish us, because we do not see what he wants to come to. But it always comes back to our own salvation.

3. **In the Spirit**

   The Spirit himself prays in us. He joins our spirit, as St Paul says, and communicates his own movement to us: the impulse of God toward us and our impulse toward God. He renews and transforms us in the image of Christ, in the communion of the Church. He sends us again toward our sisters and brothers, so that we may experience the joy of sharing with them the love that makes us live.

A trinitarian structure of prayer taking us progressively from a vague deism to a relationship with the God who revealed himself in Jesus Christ.

Identification with Christ, being turned to the Father, living from the secret dynamism of the Spirit: we think that these expressions, far from summing up a complex theory on prayer, on the contrary, designate the simplicity of the Christian experience. It is as accessible to children as it is to adults.

... Never do I say 'Father!' to God without him having first said: 'My child...'

Appropriation

Set yourself a time for prayer. Put yourself in 'a privileged relationship', in turn, with each of the divine Persons. Tell each one what you can say only to that one and not to the other Persons. Be aware of the particular way each Person refers you to the other Persons, allowing you to enter into the very heart of the mystery of God of which you have had a glimpse, which you have sensed in faith.

4. Teaching children to pray

From reading this chapter, you have probably been able to draw a few practical guidelines. Allow us to draw your attention more specifically to two very concrete ways of educating to prayer.

1. Offering the child what prepares and sustains prayer

To be sure, prayer is the profound movement of a soul turned to God. It is not up to us to intervene directly in the intimacy of this encounter. We can, on the other hand, help the child to develop certain dispositions which foster prayer:

(a) creating a material space and an environment conducive to prayer: a room or an area for prayer, various mediations (icon, cross, light...).

(b) planning specific times for prayer: either powerful moments (celebrations, recollections), or opportunities for prayer linked with the catechetic initiative (stage of interiorization, for example), or simple rituals of prayer (beginning and/or end of a session). It is important, however, that the latter be nourished by prayers freed from ritualism.

(c) exercising 'well-being' in one's body and breathing: in order to find one's spiritual setting, one must often begin by finding one's physical and corporeal place (posture, breathing).

(d) progressively exercising the attention, the faculty of recollecting oneself: dispersion and agitation of the mind will gradually yield to an interior peace, to a capacity of concentrating oneself without tension. The attention may be 'focused' on an object (a beautiful picture, for example), on an experience that we allow to echo in ourselves, on a word which has taken form, etc.

2. Putting the child in contact with the expressions of Church prayer

We must take care not to choose between formulas of prayer and spontaneous prayer, between liturgy and personal prayer, etc. These oppositions are disastrous, for prayer, on the contrary, nourishes itself on a constant to and fro motion between the spontaneous movement of the heart and the great mediations of the Church (Bible and liturgy).

In every spontaneous prayer, there should be a biblical reference (for example, a verse from a psalm, words of Jesus), and a liturgical reference (candle, cross, icon, a space set aside for prayer, etc.). Similarly, in every liturgical or official prayer, there should be room for spontaneity (this is not necessarily improvisation), a reference to actual persons who pray or celebrate, a consideration for their situation and their lives (children allowed to speak, gestures or other expressions they have chosen, etc.)

Appropriation

Keeping in mind your catecheses of the last six weeks, ask yourself to what extent you have offered the children some activities in the two areas indicated above.

48. Celebrating

The Lord Jesus... took a loaf of bread,... he broke it and said, 'This is my body that is broken for you. Do this in remembrance of me.' 1 Cor 11:23-24

To celebrate is to commemorate together an event of salvation. Let us go back to each of the elements of this definition:

1. **TO COMMEMORATE** This is about an action. Something is happening. In a specific space and time, with gestures and words, objects and movements. Not that the word is absent but it takes form. There is thus a reference to the past, to history, to something that has happened, to a reality. But the nature of memory is to make present, to actualize the experience inaugurated in the past, to make it in some way contemporary with our own time. Such an actualization gives a new impulse toward the future and confirms a promise: what has happened and what is made present, will be accomplished in the movement of the history which goes on.

2. **TOGETHER** The Church is the one celebrating, even if she is concretely represented by only a small portion of her members. This small community is the symbol – reality and sign – of the large one.

3. **EVENT OF SALVATION** Every time God and man have met in history, there has been an event of salvation; for man, salvation is, precisely, to meet this God coming to him. Among these events, some were more decisive and had a universal impact: the life, death and resurrection of Jesus Christ, foretold in the history of Israel, prolonged in the history of the Church. The focus of all celebration is the risen Christ, made present in the mystery of the Eucharist.

Together, let us become what we receive: the Body of Christ!

Appropriation

We have just defined a celebration of faith. Similar elements define a 'secular' celebration, a birthday, for example: commemorating (1), together (2), a vital event (3). Draw up a comparison between the celebration of a birthday and the celebration of Mass. In the two cases, point out the three elements of the definition: the similarities? the differences?

1. The constituents of a celebration

The structure of a celebration is simple. Everything is organized around two realities which make themselves present to each other: the community and an event of salvation.

- **The community is made present:**
  - by the physical presence of persons in the same place and at the same time;
  - by the spiritual communion of these persons among themselves. Initiating this communion is the purpose of the moments of WELCOME and RECOLLECTION (collecting our thoughts together – making the attention of everyone converge on the same point);
  - by the active participation of everyone, the exterior manifestation of the spiritual communion;
  - by taking into account the concrete historical situation of this community;
  - by the manifestation of the bond of this community (presence of a priest or another minister) with the Church.

- **The event of salvation is made present:**
  - by the Word of God which proclaims and brings into effect;
  - by one or some symbolic gesture(s) which signify it;
  - by the welcome in faith given to the Word and gestures;
  - by the profession of faith and the prayer born of this welcome.

Projected in time, this structure becomes a dynamic unfolding of which the principal phases are:

The preparation of a celebration thus consists in:

1. **identifying the community and its concrete situation;**
2. **planning the manner and the means of making it exist as community in the celebration;**
3. **identifying the event of salvation, or the aspect of this event, which will be celebrated;**
4. **planning the manner and the means of making this event present and meaningful to the community;**
5. **planning the dynamic connection of all the elements in a concrete development.**

Two basic rules to have a 'successful' celebration:

1. **In a celebration, everything must be meaningful**

Space, objects, word, silence, movements: each element contributes to create a unified world of meaningful experience.

2. **Everything must be meaningful in itself**

Commentaries and explanations are out of place here. The indispensable instructions or information are given beforehand and in a very succinct manner. Under pain of stifling the symbolism proper to the celebration. The only exception is the homily which, in direct language, clarifies a part of the meaning of the celebration – the essential.

Appropriation

With the help of this chapter, draw up a plan for the preparation of your celebration. Make a list of all the good questions to ask oneself and of all the means theoretically available to live the celebration with the children.

2. Symbolic effectiveness

The celebration being essentially a symbolic initiative, we think it is useful to deal with the question of its effectiveness, for it has one. How can its power of transformation exercised on persons and on the community be explained?

We shall consider the simple example of a symbolic object. But we remind you and stress that all the following applies above all to the living body, that of the individuals and that of the community which 'makes one body': the presence of each and the gathering are also symbolic to the highest degree.

*

On the occasion of their wedding anniversary, Nicholas offers Nathaly, his wife, a simple daisy. He has chosen this flower because, fifteen years ago, when they hardly knew each other, it was by offering a daisy during an outing that, for the first time, he made her understand: 'I love you.' This gesture, renewed today, is, we can suppose, effective and powerful. Why?

Fifteen years ago
... today...

The object offered is not just any object. It is already taken into a world of meaning, at least within the relationship Nicholas-Nathaly.

'Beyond' this object, there is Nicholas's intention, his feelings and his will, in a word, his presence.

'Before' the object, there is Nathaly' attention. She certainly sees the daisy, but she looks at it with her heart. She 'sees' Nicholas' intention.

The gift of the flower will surely become a celebration: Nicholas will not offer Nathaly his daisy in just any way, and neither will Nathaly accept it in just any way. A few gestures will be exchanged: a look, perhaps a tear, a kiss different from the others. A few words also, very simple: 'You remember... I love you...'

Result: the bond between Nathaly and Nicholas is confirmed, celebrated, reinforced, renewed, given a new start. Provided all the elements pointed out above are present. Try to remove a single one...

3. Sacramental effectiveness

In face of the power, of the effectiveness of the sacraments, two temptations continually re-emerge: to consider them as magical and technical actions ('Press on the right button and it works'), or to deny them all true efficacy by reducing them to simple ornaments ('A flower is brighter, even if it is made of plastic') or to ritual obligations ('We do not go in this restaurant without wearing a necktie!').

In reality, this is simpler and truer:

As symbolic gestures, the sacraments have the effectiveness of symbolic gestures.

They are gestures accompanying a word, sometimes an object (water, bread...), which truly become what they mean: an event of salvation. Their power is bound to the same conditions as that of any other symbolic gesture. It is the same for the sacraments as for the exchange of the flower between Nicholas and Nathaly, as for their kiss, as for their words.

There is, nonetheless, a difference. It is extraordinary. When we make symbolic gestures, our intention may be deceitful, even perverse: a bland smile to 'cheat' someone; Judas' kiss. Result: either it does not work, or else, it works in a manner contrary to what the gesture seemed to mean. Nothing of that with the sacraments:

Through the ministry of the Church, God unconditionally and totally commits himself in the sacraments. He is really 'behind' them. His intention, his presence and his will never fail nor deceive.

Because of this, the sacraments are always effective. They unconditionally offer us the life and the tender love of God. They build the Church. Even if we are not vigilant (lack of attention and faith). Even if we reject them. A true gesture of love, even rejected at the moment, remains something given. Especially if the giver has the patience of being faithful. Mothers know that very well...

Of course, this does not make faith superfluous, on the contrary. Sacraments provoke faith. Faith is another word to express this attentive love which allows the gesture to deploy all its efficacy and power. If Nathaly does not have this gaze that sees the invisible, if she has no faith, if she does not pay attention, her heart will not enter into a celebration. At least not on that day. But who knows, tomorrow? in a month?... provided Nicholas, on his part, puts up with this lack of understanding without rejecting Nathaly and having an immense hope. God is like that. Millions of times like that...

Appropriation

Use the illustration of the previous page, as well as the underlined elements, as a 'plan for the reading' of a sacrament. Similarity? difference?

4. The sacraments of Christian initiation

We propose a few complementary reflections to you, on the sacraments which are usually celebrated during the course of the children's catechesis. Our purpose is to point out their particular symbolism and to draw from them a few pedagogical guidelines.

1. BAPTISM

The fundamental experience, here, is to be reborn by symbolically living a death and a resurrection. Death to an existence under the sign of the absurd death and of sin, rebirth to a life destined to resurrection. Death to a life of isolation and birth to a life of communion. Death to a life which persists desperately and exhausts itself in vain to preserve itself, rebirth to a life which is born and reborn by giving itself. Dying to self (= dying to one's helpless and limited self), being reborn in Jesus Christ.

Water and its fluidity symbolize that very well: threatening water that can submerge us, living water where life began and where my existence developed itself for nine months.

The baptism received in the past, as a baby, underscores the gratuitous attentive love of God. He does not wait until we have reached an age when we can respond consciously to manifest to us his tender love and introduce us into the movement of his life. No more than did our parents wait for us to reach 'the years of discretion' to welcome and love us!...

This baptism, nevertheless, needs to be somewhat ratified, freely accepted by the child, the adolescent or the adult. The catechetical initiative offers privileged opportunities for that.

The baptism of children of school age, or of adolescents and adults, makes us discover again and invites us to live the whole process of conversion leading to a consciously chosen baptism.

The presence of an unbaptized child in the catechesis group can provide an opportunity for the whole group, including the baptized, to live a catechetical initiative of which the official ritual is a good reflection of its richness and pedagogy. We strongly urge you to go and see.

2. CONFIRMATION

It is often presented as the moment of commitment for the young Christian taking charge on his own of his baptism and the responsibilities flowing from it. Without minimizing this aspect in any way, we are of the opinion that it becomes meaningful only inasmuch as the confirmation is first lived as the renewal and the perfecting (the ... confirmation!) of the gift God has made at baptism. Solemn confirmation, where the Church commits herself in a particular way (presence of the bishop). A way of saying to the child or the adolescent: 'We acknowledge you to be a child of God. We confirm you in this love which was offered to you in baptism. You are important to God and to the Church.'

Pedagogically, a preparation for confirmation should, in our opinion, provide one with the opportunity to live the particular experience of being recognized in his personal and Christian identity. This experience of being accepted by an adult, by friends, in what I am, in what I carry within myself in the form of promises, is especially necessary when confirmation is celebrated during adolescence, the age par excellence for identity crises.

3. FORGIVENESS

We sometimes hesitate to celebrate this sacrament with young children for fear of 'traumatizing' them or of developing guilt feelings with respect to sin. Or, for the same reason, we are satisfied with collective celebrations because we, nevertheless, want to obey the demands made by the Church. We take the objections that can be made concerning the precocious celebrations of the sacrament of forgiveness seriously. However, it seems to us that those reticent positions concern the poorly understood celebrations and preparations, and not the reality itself.

Rather than throwing away the baby with the bath water, we are convinced that it is important to provide for the children, even if very young, this experience of a relationship which is unconditional openness: it liberates, uplifts and heals.

It appears to us even theologically clear that this experience, like that of baptism, enhances the gratuitousness of the attentive love expressed by God even before the child has been keenly aware of having freely committed a serious sin. The love of the Father is more original than the sin.

It follows, of course, that the preparation for this sacrament will not be a pedagogy of sin, but a pedagogy of mercy. That does not prevent one from speaking about sin, but without making it the centre and the major preoccupation. In the centre is Jesus Christ.

4. THE EUCHARIST

It is the sacrament of sacraments. An inexhaustible experience. We shall emphasize only one aspect, in relation with what we were saying about symbolic effectiveness. What we were stating on that subject takes a very special meaning with the Eucharist, because of Jesus' words: 'This is my body'. There is, in the Eucharist, a particularly real power. The baptismal water, for example, is not transformed (transubstantiated) like the consecrated bread. Jesus probably said, literally, according to the logic of the Aramaic language: 'This my body' (no verb to be). But the early Church understood those words in a clearly realistic sense when she translates: 'This is (and not "recalls" or "evokes") my body.' Jesus' intention was really to give in this bread his real presence as the risen Lord. The catechesis of the Eucharist should never forget that.

The mission

The Church renews herself in her activity of evangelization and catechesis. To evangelize is surely to bring the Good News and the Church to children, to young people, to adults who will thereby be enriched and renewed.

To evangelize is to give. But it is also to receive. The Church enriches and renews herself by the welcome she gives to those she has reached. To welcome children is to give them a place, to give them the freedom of the city, the right to be themselves, fully Christians, faithful to Jesus Christ in forms and ways which may be new, astonishing, even disturbing to the established ways of doing and thinking.

From the beginning, the Church has lived this experience: she has renewed herself by integrating those she has renewed through the proclamation of the gospel. Chapters 10 and 11 of the Acts of the Apostles give us a striking example of this. By opening herself to the pagans, to the non-Jews, and by welcoming them, the Christian community was forced to change, to 'de-Judaize' itself. So it was throughout history: the Church rejuvenated herself from the generous integration she offered to the newly evangelized, to those of distant lands and to the new generations. When she did not do this, for fear or out of awkwardness, she paid it dearly in loss of vitality.

The recent popes did not fail to point out this touchstone. The Church, Paul VI recalled, 'must evangelize herself by a constant conversion and renewal if she is convincingly to evangelize the world' (EN 15, cf EN 24). And John Paul II speaks of the Church as being 'the great giver as well as the great receiver of catechesis' (CT 45).

In this work, we have proposed a type of catechesis which, we believe, will bring about the renewal of the Church in its fidelity to the Tradition.

Our greatest hope is that, from a catechesis which is demanding on the part of, first, the educators and then the communities, a new sap of springtime may rise. The children to whom we will have offered Jesus Christ and the Church, in a relationship based on trust, humaneness and communion, will have aspired the breath and the fragrance of the gospel. They are the Christians of tomorrow. It will be up to them to live their faith and build the Church in a complex, difficult and unpredictable world. May we give them, not the burden of our habits, but the strength of our faith and our love. May we, from now on and within the very catechetical act, place our trust in them, accompany them and give them a taste for the gospel. Let us not have any fear. If Jesus Christ is the one we reveal to them, they have a travelling companion and a guide who knows the way.